*The*
# ORIGINS
*And*
# POWER
# OF IDEAS

## Dr. Robert Osobase

# THE ORIGINS AND POWER OF IDEAS

## Published by Cornerstone Publishing

A Division of Cornerstone Creativity Group LLC
Info@thecornerstonepublishers.com
www.thecornerstonepublishers.com

## Author's Contact

To book the author to speak at your next event or to order bulk copies of this book, please, use the information below:

**rovic72@gmail.com**

Printed in the United States of America.

# DEDICATION

For my wife, Victoria

# CONTENTS

DEDICATION ............................................................ ii

ACKNOWLEDGMENTS ......................................... v

INTRODUCTION ................................................. vii

1. The Birth of Ideas ......................................... 1

2. The Evolution of Ideas ................................. 19

3. The Influence of Ideas on Society ............... 37

4. Ideas that Changed the World ..................... 55

5. The Power of Disruptive Ideas .................... 81

6. The Role of Ideas in Problem-Solving ....... 87

7. Harnessing the Power of Ideas ................... 93

8. Ideas and Personal Growth ....................... 103

9. Ideas and Innovation in the Digital Age .... 121

10. Ideas and Social Change ........................... 127

11. Ideas and Global Collaboration ................ 133

12. The Future of Ideas .................................. 139

CONCLUSION ...................................................... 145

ABOUT THE AUTHOR ...................................... 149

# ACKNOWLEDGMENTS

Writing a book is a journey that cannot be undertaken alone. It requires the support, encouragement, and guidance of numerous individuals who contribute their time, expertise, and unwavering belief in the project. It is with profound gratitude that I acknowledge their invaluable contributions to the creation of this book.

First and foremost, I would like to express my deepest appreciation to my family. They have been my pillars of strength throughout this endeavor, providing constant love, support, and understanding. Their unwavering belief in me and their sacrifices made it possible for me to dedicate the necessary time and effort to bringing this book to life.

I am deeply indebted to my brother-in-law, John Agboifoh who stood by me during the highs and lows of the writing process. His enthusiasm, feedback, and encouragement were instrumental in keeping me motivated and focused.

Additionally, I express my appreciation to the publishing team at Amazon Kindle Direct Publishing. Their dedication, professionalism, and belief in this project have been integral to its success. Their tireless efforts in editing, design, marketing, and distribution have transformed this manuscript into a book that I am proud to call my own.

Finally, I am indebted to the countless readers and supporters who have embraced my work. Your enthusiasm and encouragement have been a constant source of inspiration, and I am humbled by your unwavering support.

To everyone who has played a part, big or small, in the creation of this book, I extend my deepest gratitude. Your contributions have made this journey not only possible but also immensely rewarding. Thank you for being a part of this endeavor and for helping me bring this book into the world.

With heartfelt appreciation,

Robert Osobase

# INTRODUCTION

Ideas have the extraordinary ability to shape our world, revolutionize societies, and transform the course of human history. They are the ethereal seeds that sprout in the fertile soil of our minds, giving birth to innovation, progress, and change. From the humblest of beginnings to the grandest of achievements, ideas have been the driving force behind remarkable feats, be they scientific breakthroughs, artistic masterpieces, or social movements that challenge the status quo. Ideas are the lifeblood of human progress. They shape our understanding, drive innovation, and fuel creativity. But where do these ideas come from? How do they emerge within the confines of our minds, seemingly out of thin air?

Throughout the ages, the power of ideas has been evident in the lives of great thinkers, philosophers, inventors, and visionaries who dared to dream beyond the boundaries of conventionality. It was through the power of ideas that Galileo Galilei challenged the geocentric view of the universe, setting in motion the scientific revolution. It was through the power of ideas that Martin Luther King Jr. envisioned a world free from racial discrimination, sparking the civil rights movement. And it was through the power of ideas that Leonardo da Vinci sketched his ingenious designs, foreshadowing modern inventions centuries before their time.

Ideas possess a unique quality—they are intangible, yet possess the ability to inspire, influence, and ignite action. They are not bound by physical limitations or constrained by borders. Ideas traverse oceans and continents, spreading like wildfire as they capture the hearts and minds of individuals. The power of an idea lies not in its confinement, but in its ability to resonate with others, to provoke contemplation and discussion, and to incite positive change.

In today's interconnected world, the power of ideas has only amplified. With the advent of technology and the rise of social media platforms, ideas can now be shared instantaneously and reach vast audiences with unprecedented speed. The barriers to entry have been lowered, empowering individuals from all social classes to contribute their unique perspectives and challenge prevailing narratives.

However, the power of ideas is a double-edged sword. While ideas have the potential to inspire progress, they can also be used to propagate misinformation, division, and harmful ideologies. It is crucial, now more than ever, to cultivate a critical and discerning mindset, to question and evaluate the ideas that surround us, and to harness the power of ideas for the greater good.

In this exploration of "The Origins and Power of Ideas,"

we will delve into the profound influence ideas have on our lives and society. We will examine how ideas shape our beliefs, fuel innovation, and shape cultural and societal norms. We will also confront the challenges that arise when ideas clash and the responsibility we hold as individuals to engage in thoughtful discourse and contribute positively to the world of ideas.

Join us on this intellectual journey as we unravel the mysteries, celebrate the triumphs, and navigate the complexities of the power of ideas. Together, let us uncover the transformative potential that lies within the realm of our thoughts, and harness this power to shape a brighter future for ourselves and generations to come.

# CHAPTER 1

# THE BIRTH
# OF IDEAS

The birth of ideas is a fascinating and complex process. It involves the formation and development of new concepts, thoughts, and perspectives that can lead to innovative solutions, creativity, and progress in various fields. While the exact mechanisms behind idea generation are not fully understood, there are several factors and processes that are commonly associated with the birth of ideas.

# INSPIRATION

The phenomenon of inspiration or sudden insights provides us with some insight into the origin of ideas. These can be triggered by a wide range of stimuli, such as observing the world around us, encountering problems or challenges, engaging in discussions or brainstorming sessions, or even through introspection and contemplation. Inspiration, in its simplest form, refers to the sudden influx of creative thoughts or insights. It is often described as a spark, a moment of clarity that illuminates the mind and sets the wheels of creativity in motion. The concept of inspiration has fascinated philosophers, artists, and scientists throughout history, as it holds the key to unlocking the mysteries of human imagination.

One prevailing theory on the origin of ideas by inspiration suggests that they arise from the depths of our subconscious mind. Our subconscious is a reservoir of thoughts, memories, and experiences that are not immediately accessible to our conscious awareness. It is a realm of untapped potential, waiting to be harnessed.

When we encounter a problem or engage in creative pursuits, our conscious mind grapples with the challenge at hand. We may consciously explore various avenues and possibilities, but it is often the subconscious mind that holds the key to unlocking a breakthrough. In these moments, inspiration acts as a bridge between our conscious and subconscious minds, allowing ideas to flow freely.

Inspiration can be triggered by a multitude of stimuli. It may be sparked by an observation, a conversation, a piece of art, or even a fleeting moment of introspection. These triggers serve as catalysts, activating the subconscious and setting off a chain reaction of associative thinking. As our subconscious mind connects seemingly disparate pieces of information, new ideas begin to take shape.

Another perspective on the origin of ideas by inspiration lies in the notion of interconnectedness. According to this view, ideas do not emerge solely from within an individual's mind but are influenced by the collective consciousness of society. We are all products of our cultural, social, and intellectual environments, and our ideas are deeply entwined with the ideas of others.

Inspiration, in this sense, becomes a conduit through which we tap into the collective wisdom and knowledge of humanity. It is through exposure to diverse perspectives, experiences, and disciplines that we broaden our intellectual horizons and invite new ideas to take root. By engaging with the ideas of others, we become part of an ongoing dialogue that transcends time and space.

The origin of ideas by inspiration is a complex and multifaceted process. It encompasses both the individual and the collective, the conscious and the subconscious, the known and the unknown. It is a delicate dance between the familiar and the novel, the rational and the intuitive.

To nurture inspiration and foster the emergence of new ideas, it is essential to create an environment that encourages curiosity, exploration, and open-mindedness. By embracing a spirit of intellectual curiosity and actively seeking out diverse sources of inspiration, we can unlock the potential of our minds and tap into the wellspring of creativity that lies within us.

The origin of ideas by inspiration is a fascinating and elusive phenomenon. It arises from the depths of our subconscious mind, fueled by our experiences, observations, and interactions with the world. It is influenced by the collective consciousness of society and thrives in an environment that fosters curiosity and open-mindedness. By embracing inspiration and harnessing its power, we can unlock the boundless potential of human imagination and propel ourselves towards new frontiers of knowledge and innovation.

## KNOWLEDGE AND EXPERIENCE

Two significant factors that contribute to the origin of ideas are knowledge and experiences that individuals possess. Knowledge refers to the information, understanding, and skills that a person possesses. It is acquired through learning, education, and exposure to various sources of information such as books, lectures, conversations, and observations. Knowledge provides the foundation for generating and developing ideas. When we encounter new information, we connect it with our existing knowledge, allowing us to make associations, draw conclusions, and generate new ideas. The more extensive and diverse our knowledge base, the more material we must draw upon when generating ideas.

Experience, on the other hand, refers to the direct encounter with the world through our senses. It encompasses our interactions with the physical environment, other people, and the events and situations we go through. Experience provides us with firsthand information and sensory inputs that can shape our thoughts, perceptions, and ideas.

Through experience, we gather data, make observations, and learn from the consequences of our actions. This accumulation of experiences helps us form new connections, identify patterns, and generate novel ideas.

Knowledge and experience are interconnected and mutually reinforced. Our knowledge informs our experiences, and our experiences, in turn, enrich and expand our knowledge. They work together in a continuous cycle, influencing and shaping the origin of ideas.

It's worth noting that the creative process involves more than just knowledge and experience. Other factors, such as imagination, intuition, and cognitive processes, also play significant roles in generating ideas. However, knowledge and experience provide the raw materials and the context within which these other factors operate.

Ultimately, one of the origins of ideas is a complex interplay of knowledge and experience, combined with various cognitive processes and creative abilities. The acquisition of knowledge and the accumulation of experiences fuel our thinking, stimulate our imagination, and provide the building blocks for generating innovative and meaningful ideas.

The more diverse and extensive one's knowledge base, the more connections and associations can be made between different concepts, leading to the emergence of novel ideas. Therefore, continuously learning, exploring different fields, and acquiring a broad range of experiences can enhance the generation of ideas.

## ASSOCIATIVE THINKING

Associative thinking is a cognitive process through which ideas or concepts are connected or linked together based on their similarities, contrasts, or any other meaningful relationships. It involves making connections between different pieces of information stored in our memory and using those connections to generate innovative ideas or insights.

The origin of ideas through associative thinking can be traced back to various psychological and philosophical theories. One prominent theory is that of associationism, which suggests that the mind organizes information by forming associations between related ideas. This theory has its roots in the works of philosophers like John Locke, David Hume, and John Stuart Mill.

According to associationism, ideas are initially acquired through sensory experiences and stored in the mind as discrete elements. These elements are then connected through various associations, such as similarities, contiguity, cause and effect, or other relationships. When we encounter a stimulus or a trigger, it activates a network of associated ideas, leading to the emergence of new thoughts or concepts.

For example, imagine you see a picture of a cat. This visual stimulus activates a network of associated ideas, such as the concept of animals, pets, fur, or the sound of a meow. These associations may further trigger related ideas like the notion of domestication, different breeds of cats, or even broader topics like the history of cats in diverse cultures. Through associative thinking, you can generate innovative ideas or connections based on these associations.

Associative thinking can be enhanced through techniques such as brainstorming, mind mapping, or free association exercises. These methods aim to promote the generation of ideas by encouraging the exploration of various associations and connections. By allowing the mind to freely roam through different concepts and linking them together, creative insights can emerge.

It is important to note that associative thinking is not limited to conscious, deliberate processes. Our minds naturally make connections between ideas even without explicit intention. This is why sometimes ideas seem to "pop up" in our minds seemingly out of nowhere. Our brains continuously work to form associations and retrieve relevant information, leading to the spontaneous emergence of innovative ideas or insights.

The origin of ideas through associative thinking can be attributed to the innate cognitive process of forming associations between related concepts. By connecting different pieces of information in our minds, we can generate innovative ideas, solve problems, and foster creativity. Associative thinking is a fundamental aspect of human cognition and plays a significant role in the creative process.

## PROBLEM-SOLVING AND CREATIVITY

Many ideas are born out of the need to solve problems or address challenges. This process often involves thinking critically, analyzing the existing situation, and seeking alternative solutions.

The origin of ideas through problem-solving and creativity is a fascinating aspect of human cognition. Both problem-solving and creativity are cognitive processes that involve the generation of novel and valuable ideas or solutions. While they are distinct processes, they often overlap and interact with each other.

Problem-solving refers to the cognitive process of finding solutions to specific challenges or obstacles. It involves identifying the problem, analyzing its components, and applying relevant knowledge and strategies to arrive at a solution. Problem-solving can be approached systematically, using logical reasoning and deductive thinking, or it can involve more intuitive and trial-and-error methods.

Creativity, on the other hand, is the ability to generate novel and valuable ideas, concepts, or solutions that are often beyond conventional or established thinking patterns. It involves the ability to think divergently, make new connections, and explore alternative perspectives. Creativity is not limited to any specific domain and can manifest in various forms, such as artistic expression, scientific discoveries, technological innovations, or problem-solving approaches.

The process of generating ideas through problem-solving often involves a combination of analytical thinking and creative thinking. Analytical thinking helps in understanding the problem, breaking it down into manageable components, and identifying potential solutions based on existing knowledge and logical reasoning. Creative thinking, on the other hand, enables individuals to think beyond conventional boundaries, explore unconventional solutions, and make novel connections between seemingly unrelated concepts.

Creativity can play a crucial role in problem-solving by enabling individuals to approach problems from different angles and come up with innovative solutions. It allows for the exploration of alternative perspectives, consideration of multiple variables, and the generation of out-of-the-box ideas that may not have been considered otherwise.

Problem-solving and creativity are not entirely independent processes. In fact, they often complement and enhance each other. When faced with a problem, individuals may employ creative thinking techniques to generate a wide range of possible solutions. These solutions can then be evaluated and refined using analytical thinking to determine their feasibility and effectiveness.

It's important to note that both problem-solving and creativity can be cultivated and developed through various strategies and practices. Engaging in activities that promote critical thinking, embracing diverse perspectives, encouraging curiosity, and fostering an environment that values and supports creative thinking can all contribute to the origin of innovative ideas.

The origin of ideas through problem-solving and creativity involves a dynamic interplay between analytical thinking and creative thinking. Problem-solving provides the framework and structure to address specific challenges, while creativity expands the possibilities and generates novel and valuable solutions. Together, they form a powerful cognitive process that fuels innovation and drives human progress.

## COLLABORATION AND FEEDBACK

Ideas can be refined and expanded through collaboration with others. By sharing ideas, engaging in discussions, and receiving feedback, individuals can gain new insights, perspectives, and suggestions that can further develop and improve their initial concepts.

The origin of ideas through collaboration and feedback is a fascinating aspect of human creativity and innovation. While individuals can certainly come up with innovative ideas on their own, the power of collaboration and feedback often leads to the development of more refined and impactful concepts.

When people collaborate, they bring together their unique perspectives, knowledge, skills, and experiences. This diversity of inputs can spark new connections and combinations of ideas that may not have emerged otherwise. Through brainstorming sessions, discussions, and open dialogue, collaborators can build upon each other's ideas, challenge assumptions, and explore new possibilities.

Feedback also plays a crucial role in shaping and refining ideas. By sharing ideas with others and receiving their input, individuals gain valuable insights, alternative viewpoints, and constructive criticism. Feedback helps identify potential flaws, highlights strengths, and provides suggestions for improvement. This iterative process of sharing ideas, receiving feedback, and incorporating changes leads to the evolution and enhancement of concepts.

Collaboration and feedback also foster a culture of innovation and continuous learning. When people work together and exchange feedback, they create an environment that encourages exploration, risk-taking, and the sharing of diverse perspectives. This collaborative culture nurtures creativity and stimulates the generation of new ideas.

In many fields, such as science, technology, and the arts, collaboration and feedback are integral to the creative process. Scientific researchers collaborate to design experiments, share data, and collectively analyze results. Artists and designers often seek feedback from their peers or audiences to refine their work. In the business world, teams collaborate on projects, share ideas, and iterate based on feedback to develop innovative products and services.

Collaboration and feedback can occur through various channels, including face-to-face meetings, group discussions, online platforms, and even anonymous feedback mechanisms. Advancements in technology and communication have further expanded opportunities for global collaboration, enabling people from different locations to connect and share ideas effortlessly.

It is important to note that collaboration and feedback are not guaranteed to lead to successful ideas every time. However, by embracing a collaborative mindset and actively seeking feedback, individuals and teams increase their chances of generating novel, well-rounded, and impactful ideas. The iterative nature of collaboration and feedback allows for continuous improvement and the refinement of ideas over time.

Overall, the origin of ideas through collaboration and feedback demonstrates the power of collective intelligence and the synergistic effect of diverse perspectives. By harnessing the collective wisdom of a group, individuals can push the boundaries of creativity, refine their ideas, and bring forth innovative solutions to complex problems.

## ENVIRONMENT AND CULTURE

The environment plays a significant role in shaping our ideas. Our surroundings, including the physical space we inhabit and the natural world around us, can inspire and influence the way we think. For example, exposure to different landscapes, such as mountains, forests, or oceans, can evoke certain emotions and stimulate creative thinking. Similarly, urban environments with their vibrant cultures, diverse populations, and technological advancements can foster innovation and provide fertile ground for innovative ideas to emerge.

Moreover, the environment provides us with experiences

and stimuli that spark ideas. Interactions with people, objects, and events shape our perspectives and contribute to the formation of new thoughts. For instance, travel to different countries exposes us to diverse cultures, traditions, and ways of life, expanding our horizons and inspiring fresh ideas. Likewise, engaging in outdoor activities, participating in social events, or even observing everyday situations can trigger unique insights and perspectives.

Culture, on the other hand, refers to the shared beliefs, values, customs, and behaviors of a particular group of people. It encompasses aspects such as language, religion, arts, social norms, and historical traditions. Culture has a profound impact on the origin of ideas as it shapes our worldview and influences the way we interpret and understand the world around us.

Within a specific culture, ideas are transmitted through various means, including storytelling, literature, art, music, and oral traditions. These cultural expressions not only reflect the existing ideas within a society but also serve as a source of inspiration for innovative ideas. They provide a platform for sharing knowledge, challenging established norms, and fostering creativity.

Furthermore, cultural diversity plays a crucial role in the origin of ideas. When diverse cultures interact and exchange ideas, there is an opportunity for cross-pollination of thoughts and the emergence of innovative concepts.

This can occur through cultural exchange, migration, globalization, and the advancement of technology, which enable easier communication and sharing of ideas across borders.

It is important to note that while the environment and culture significantly influence the origin of ideas, they are not the sole determinants. Individual factors such as subjective experiences, cognitive processes, education, and genetics also contribute to the formation of ideas.

The origin of ideas is a dynamic process influenced by the environment and culture. The environment provides stimuli and experiences that spark new thoughts, while culture shapes our worldview and serves as a source of inspiration. The interplay between these factors, along with individual differences, contributes to the rich tapestry of ideas that shape our societies.

It is important to note that the birth of ideas is a dynamic and iterative process. Ideas can evolve, transform, and merge with other ideas, leading to the emergence of even more complex and groundbreaking concepts. Moreover, the implementation and realization of ideas often require further development, refinement, and practical considerations. Nonetheless, the birth of ideas serves as a fundamental catalyst for progress and innovation in various aspects of human endeavor.

Ideas are the cornerstone of human progress. They

shape our understanding of the world, ignite imagination, and inspire action. From scientific breakthroughs to philosophical paradigms, ideas have played a fundamental role in driving societal advancement throughout history.

The origins of ideas are diverse and can emerge from a myriad of sources. They can be sparked by observation, curiosity, necessity, or even serendipity. Some ideas are born out of individual brilliance, while others are the result of collaborative efforts or the cumulative knowledge of preceding generations. Ideas can arise from subjective experiences, cultural influences, or the challenges faced by societies.

Once an idea takes root, its impact on society can be profound. Ideas have the power to challenge existing norms, provoke critical thinking, and ignite intellectual debates. They can reshape our understanding of reality, redefine social structures, and drive technological innovation. Whether it is the Copernican heliocentric model, the theory of evolution, or the concept of democracy, ideas have transformed the course of human history.

One of the remarkable aspects of ideas is their ability to transcend time and space. They can traverse borders, cultures, and generations, influencing societies far beyond their inception. The spread of ideas has been facilitated by various means, such as writing, oral tradition, and, more recently, the internet. The printing press, for instance, played a pivotal role in disseminating ideas during the Renaissance and the scientific revolution, enabling the spread of knowledge, and sparking an intellectual revolution.

Ideas have the potential to inspire and motivate individuals and communities. They can fuel social movements, incite political revolutions, and advocate for justice and equality. Thinkers like Karl Marx, Martin Luther King Jr., and Mary Wollstonecraft have introduced ideas that have galvanized masses and fueled transformative movements.

Moreover, ideas can drive scientific progress, leading to breakthroughs and innovations that improve our lives. From the discovery of electricity to the development of vaccines, ideas have propelled scientific advancements that have revolutionized our understanding of the natural world and enhanced human well-being.

However, it is important to recognize that not all ideas are positive or beneficial. Ideas can be used to propagate harmful ideologies, incite violence, or perpetuate inequality. History is replete with instances where ideas have been exploited to justify oppression, discrimination, and war. Therefore, critical evaluation and ethical considerations are essential when assessing the impact of ideas on society.

In conclusion, ideas are the catalysts of human progress. They shape our societies, drive change, and inspire us to push the boundaries of knowledge. The origins of ideas are diverse, and their impact can be far-reaching, transforming social, cultural, and scientific landscapes. As we navigate the future, fostering an environment that nurtures and embraces innovative ideas will continue to be essential for the advancement of humanity.

# CHAPTER 2
# THE EVOLUTION
# OF IDEAS

The evolution of ideas refers to the process by which concepts, theories, and beliefs change and develop over time. Ideas can evolve through various mechanisms, including cultural shifts, scientific advancements, social movements, and individual contributions. Let us explore the evolution of ideas in more detail:

## CULTURAL AND HISTORICAL CONTEXT

Ideas are shaped by the cultural and historical context in which they emerge. Societal values, norms, and beliefs heavily influence the development and acceptance of innovative ideas. Over time, as cultures change and adapt, so do the ideas that govern them. Ideas are not static entities but rather dynamic and fluid, shaped by the societies, cultures, and historical periods in which they emerge and develop. Let's explore how cultural and historical contexts shape the evolution of ideas.

Cultural context encompasses the beliefs, values, norms, traditions, and practices of a particular society or group. These elements play a crucial role in shaping and influencing ideas. Cultural context provides a framework through which individuals perceive the world and interpret added information. It establishes the boundaries of what is considered acceptable or taboo, shapes perspectives on morality, and influences how ideas are transmitted and received within a community.

For example, consider the concept of individualism versus collectivism. In Western cultures, individualism is highly valued, and ideas promoting personal freedom and autonomy are often celebrated. In contrast, many Eastern cultures emphasize collectivism and prioritize community well-being over individual desires. This cultural context significantly influences the evolution of ideas related to governance, social relationships, and personal identity.

Historical context refers to the specific historical period in which ideas emerge and develop. Historical events, social movements, technological advancements, and political changes all contribute to the evolution of ideas. Historical context shapes the concerns, challenges, and aspirations of a society, providing a backdrop against which ideas are formulated and debated.

For instance, the Enlightenment era of the 18th century was a time of significant intellectual and philosophical development. Ideas such as reason, human rights, and democracy emerged as a response to the oppressive monarchies of the time. The historical context of political revolutions, scientific discoveries, and the spread of literacy played a vital role in the evolution of these ideas, which laid the foundation for modern democratic societies.

Cultural and historical contexts are intricately intertwined, and their interplay further shapes the evolution of ideas. Cultural values and traditions influence how historical events are interpreted and understood. At the same time, historical events and social changes can challenge existing cultural norms and lead to the emergence of new ideas.

For example, the feminist movement of the 20th century emerged in response to historical events such as the suffrage movement and the changing roles of women during World War II. The movement challenged traditional gender roles and advocated for women's rights, leading to significant shifts in societal attitudes and the evolution of ideas related to gender equality.

It's important to recognize that the evolution of ideas is

not linear but rather complex and multifaceted. Ideas are influenced by a range of factors, including cultural and historical contexts, as well as individual experiences and interactions. Understanding the interplay between cultural and historical contexts provides valuable insights into how ideas evolve and transform over time.

## SCIENTIFIC ADVANCEMENTS

The evolution of ideas is intricately linked to scientific advancements throughout history. Scientific discoveries and progress have consistently challenged and transformed our understanding of the world, leading to the emergence of the latest ideas and paradigms. Let's explore how scientific advancements have shaped the evolution of ideas in various fields.

Scientific advancements in cosmology and astronomy have revolutionized our understanding of the universe. From the geocentric model proposed by Ptolemy to the heliocentric model proposed by Copernicus, scientific observations and measurements have debunked old ideas and provided a more accurate understanding of our place in the cosmos. Further discoveries, such as Edwin Hubble's observation of the expanding universe, the discovery of cosmic microwave background radiation, and the identification of exoplanets, have continued to reshape our cosmic perspective.

Charles Darwin's theory of evolution by natural selection, based on his observations during the voyage of the HMS

Beagle, challenged prevailing ideas about the origin and diversity of species. Darwin's work, supported by subsequent scientific discoveries in genetics and paleontology, provided a unifying framework that explained the complexity of life on Earth. Advances in genetics, DNA sequencing, and molecular biology have further expanded our understanding of evolution and led to the development of the modern synthesis of evolutionary biology.

Scientific advancements have revolutionized medical practices and healthcare outcomes. From the discovery and development of antibiotics to the understanding of DNA's structure and function, scientific breakthroughs have paved the way for improved diagnostics, treatments, and preventive measures. Techniques such as vaccination, organ transplantation, and minimally invasive surgeries have transformed medical practices, prolonging and improving the quality of life for countless individuals.

The field of physics has witnessed numerous scientific advancements that have challenged and expanded our understanding of the fundamental laws of nature. From Isaac Newton's laws of motion and gravity to Albert Einstein's theory of relativity, these breakthroughs have revolutionized our understanding of space, time, and energy. The advent of quantum mechanics, with its probabilistic nature and wave-particle duality, has introduced a new paradigm that has reshaped our understanding of the microscopic world and led to groundbreaking technologies such as transistors and lasers.

23

Scientific advancements in information and communication technology have transformed the way we exchange and access knowledge. The development of the telegraph, telephone, and internet has revolutionized communication, enabling real-time global connectivity. Breakthroughs in computer science, such as the invention of the transistor, integrated circuits, and the development of algorithms, have led to the creation of powerful computers and the birth of the digital age.

These are just a few examples of how scientific advancements have influenced the evolution of ideas. Scientific progress has consistently challenged established beliefs, expanded our knowledge, and sparked new avenues of inquiry. As technology and scientific understanding continue to advance, we can expect further transformative shifts in our understanding of the world and the emergence of innovative ideas.

## SOCIAL MOVEMENTS AND ACTIVISM

The evolution of ideas by social movements and activism is a complex and dynamic process that has played a crucial role throughout history in driving social and political change. Social movements and activism are born out of a collective desire for change and are driven by a range of factors, such as grievances, aspirations for justice, and a desire to challenge existing power structures and norms.

Social movements often emerge in response to perceived injustices or grievances within society. These can be related to issues such as civil rights, gender equality, environmental degradation, economic inequality, or any other form of social or political oppression. Activists and movements identify these problems and recognize the need for change.

Once a grievance is identified, activists and organizers work to mobilize individuals and communities to take collective action. This can involve organizing protests, demonstrations, strikes, boycotts, or other forms of nonviolent resistance. The aim is to raise awareness about the issue and build a critical mass of support.

Social movements and activists strive to shape public opinion by highlighting the injustices and advocating for their cause. They employ various strategies to disseminate information, engage with the media, use social networks, and employ storytelling techniques to raise awareness and generate empathy and support for their cause. This helps in building a broader base of supporters and allies.

Social movements often challenge the existing power structures and systems that perpetuate injustice. They confront governments, institutions, corporations, or any other entities that maintain the status quo. Movements may demand policy changes, legal reforms, or institutional transformations to address the grievances and achieve their goals.

As social movements progress, ideas and strategies evolve. Activists engage in dialogue, debate, and collective reflection to refine their goals and tactics. They learn from past experiences and adapt their approaches based on successes and failures. Innovative ideas, ideologies, and frameworks may emerge as movements gain momentum and engage with a wider range of perspectives.

Social movements often recognize the importance of building coalitions and forging alliances with other groups that share common values or face similar forms of oppression. Intersectionality, which acknowledges the interconnected nature of different forms of discrimination, becomes a prominent factor in the evolution of ideas. Movements increasingly embrace diversity and inclusivity to build stronger and more effective movements.

Successful social movements can bring about significant societal change. They can influence public policy, create new laws, challenge social norms, and shape cultural attitudes. Over time, the impact of these changes can be seen in various areas, including human rights, labor rights, environmental protection, gender and racial equality, LGBTQ+ rights, and many others.

Social movements leave a legacy by inspiring and influencing future generations of activists. The ideas, strategies, and lessons learned from past movements become part of a collective knowledge that informs and guides future movements. Movements often build upon the achievements of their predecessors and continue the struggle for justice and equality.

It is important to note that the evolution of ideas by social movements and activism is not a linear process, and it can vary significantly depending on the context, culture, and specific issues involved. Additionally, different movements employ diverse strategies and tactics based on their goals, resources, and the socio-political environment they operate in.

## INTERDISCIPLINARY APPROACHES

The exchange of ideas across disciplines can fuel their evolution. Interdisciplinary collaboration allows concepts and theories from different fields to intersect, leading to innovative ideas and approaches. Integrating knowledge and methods from multiple disciplines allows one to gain a deeper understanding of complex problems and develop innovative solutions. It involves breaking down traditional disciplinary boundaries and fostering collaboration and exchange between different fields of study.

Interdisciplinary approaches recognize that many real-world problems are multifaceted and cannot be adequately addressed by a single discipline alone. By bringing together insights from diverse areas, such as science, technology, engineering, arts, humanities, social sciences, and more, interdisciplinary approaches aim to generate new perspectives, theories, and methodologies that can lead to breakthroughs in understanding and problem-solving.

Interdisciplinary approaches allow for a more comprehensive understanding of complex phenomena by incorporating multiple viewpoints and knowledge bases. This can lead to a more nuanced analysis of problems and uncover hidden connections that may not be apparent within a single discipline.

The convergence of different disciplines often sparks creativity and innovation. When experts from different fields collaborate, they can bring together unique insights, methodologies, and approaches, leading to the development of novel ideas and solutions.

Interdisciplinary approaches can bridge gaps between different fields of study, enabling the transfer of knowledge, concepts, and methods. This facilitates cross-fertilization of ideas and promotes a more integrated and interconnected body of knowledge.

Many of the pressing challenges facing society today, such as climate change, poverty, and healthcare, require interdisciplinary approaches. These problems are multifaceted and cannot be adequately addressed by a single discipline. By combining expertise from various disciplines, interdisciplinary approaches offer a more comprehensive framework for understanding and addressing complex problems.

Interdisciplinary approaches foster collaboration and cooperation among experts from different fields. This collaborative spirit encourages the sharing of knowledge, expertise, and resources, leading to a more effective and holistic problem-solving process.

Interdisciplinary approaches also consider the ethical, cultural, and social dimensions of ideas and their implications. By incorporating diverse perspectives, interdisciplinary research helps to ensure that ideas and innovations are ethically sound, culturally sensitive, and socially responsible.

However, interdisciplinary approaches also face challenges, including the need for effective communication and coordination among disciplines, addressing differences in terminology and methodology, and fostering a supportive institutional framework that values and promotes interdisciplinary research.

The evolution of ideas through interdisciplinary approaches holds great promise for advancing knowledge, addressing complex problems, and driving innovation. By breaking down disciplinary silos and promoting collaboration, interdisciplinary approaches can lead to transformative discoveries and insights that have a positive impact on society.

# TECHNOLOGICAL ADVANCEMENTS

Technological advancements have played a significant role in shaping the evolution of ideas throughout human history. From the invention of writing and the printing press to the development of the internet and artificial intelligence, technology has revolutionized the way we communicate, access information, and interact with the world.

The invention of writing and later the printing press made it possible to record and disseminate knowledge and ideas more efficiently. This led to the preservation and spread of information across time and space, enabling the accumulation of knowledge and the development of new ideas. The advent of the internet and digital communication technologies further accelerated the exchange of information, connecting people from different parts of the world and facilitating the rapid dissemination of ideas.

Technology has democratized access to knowledge and information. In the past, access to education and scholarly resources was limited to a privileged few. However, with the rise of technologies like the internet, e-books, and online courses, information has become more accessible to a larger portion of the population. This has empowered individuals to explore new ideas, engage in self-learning, and contribute to intellectual discourse.

Technological advancements have facilitated collaborative creation and crowdsourcing of ideas. Platforms like

Wikipedia, open-source software, and social media have enabled people to collaborate and contribute their knowledge, insights, and ideas on a global scale. This has led to the emergence of collective intelligence, where diverse perspectives and expertise can converge to solve complex problems and drive innovation.

Technological advancements have disrupted traditional industries and paradigms, forcing societies to adapt and embrace new ideas. For example, the advent of digital music distribution revolutionized the music industry, challenging traditional business models and leading to the emergence of new ways of creating, distributing, and consuming music. Similarly, technologies like blockchain, 3D printing, and renewable energy are challenging established systems and prompting the exploration of alternative ideas and approaches.

The development of artificial intelligence (AI) and automation technologies has raised profound questions about the future of work, ethics, and the nature of human intelligence. AI has the potential to automate routine tasks, freeing up human creativity and cognitive abilities for more complex problem-solving and idea generation. It also presents challenges related to job displacement and ethical considerations, spurring debates, and discussions on the impact of technology on society.

Overall, technological advancements have been instrumental in shaping the evolution of ideas by facilitating communication, democratizing knowledge, enabling collaboration, disrupting industries, and challenging existing paradigms. As technology continues to advance, it will undoubtedly continue to shape and influence the way we think, create, and interact with ideas in the future.

## INDIVIDUAL CONTRIBUTIONS

Ideas can also evolve through the contributions of individuals. Thinkers, philosophers, scientists, and artists have played a crucial role in shaping and challenging existing ideas. Their unique perspectives, discoveries, and creations have often sparked intellectual revolutions and paradigm shifts. Ideas rarely emerge fully formed; instead, they develop and evolve through a collaborative and cumulative process.

Every idea starts with an individual or a small group of people who come up with an initial concept or insight. This seed of an idea can be sparked by personal experiences, observations, or a desire to solve a particular problem. Once the initial idea is conceived, it typically undergoes expansion and development through the contributions of other individuals. These contributors may be colleagues, collaborators, or even critics who provide feedback, suggestions, and alternative perspectives. Their input helps refine and shape the idea, leading to its growth and maturation.

As the idea develops, individuals start applying and

experimenting with it in various contexts. This process involves testing the feasibility, effectiveness, and practicality of the idea. By implementing the concept in real-world scenarios, individuals can gain valuable insights and make necessary adjustments or improvements.

Ideas rarely emerge as perfect solutions right away. They often require multiple iterations and refinements to reach their full potential. Individual contributors play a crucial role in this process by critically evaluating the idea, identifying flaws or limitations, and suggesting modifications or enhancements. Each iteration builds upon the previous one, gradually shaping the idea into a more robust and refined form.

Ideas evolve and spread through communication and dissemination. Individual contributors share their ideas through various mediums, such as publications, presentations, conversations, or digital platforms. This dissemination allows others to learn about the idea, engage with it, and contribute further, thus extending its influence and impact.

Ideas often intertwine and intersect with other ideas, leading to the emergence of new concepts or frameworks. Individual contributors who engage with multiple disciplines or fields of study can integrate ideas from various sources, synthesizing them into novel and innovative frameworks. This cross-pollination of ideas fosters interdisciplinary collaboration and drives further evolution.

The contributions made by individuals to the evolution of ideas create a legacy. Ideas that have a profound impact can shape the course of human knowledge, influence future generations, and become the foundation for new ideas and discoveries. The collective contributions of individuals over time form the intellectual heritage that guides and inspires future thinkers and innovators.

It is important to note that the evolution of ideas is not always linear or straightforward. Ideas can face resistance, controversy, and backlash before they gain acceptance and become mainstream. Additionally, the evolution of ideas is an ongoing process, and innovative ideas continue to emerge, challenging and building upon existing ones.

Overall, the evolution of ideas is a dynamic and complex phenomenon influenced by a range of factors, including cultural context, scientific progress, social movements, interdisciplinary collaboration, technological advancements, and individual contributions. It reflects the ever-changing nature of human knowledge and our collective quest for understanding and improvement.

Examining how ideas evolve and adapt over time requires an understanding of the interplay between ideas and the cultural, social, and technological changes that shape our world. Ideas are not static entities but are influenced by and influence the context in which they exist.

Cultural changes, such as shifts in values, beliefs, and norms, can significantly impact the evolution of ideas. As societies change, new perspectives and worldviews emerge, leading to the reevaluation and reinterpretation of existing ideas. For example, societal movements advocating for gender equality have influenced the evolution of ideas related to gender roles, leading to changes in social norms and expectations.

Social changes, including demographic shifts and changes in power dynamics, also play a crucial role in the evolution of ideas. As societies become more diverse, ideas from diverse cultures and backgrounds interact and blend, leading to the emergence of new perspectives and hybrid ideas. Additionally, social movements and collective actions can challenge existing ideas and foster the development of alternative concepts and ideologies.

Technological advancements have a profound impact on the evolution of ideas. Modern technologies enable the dissemination of information, facilitate communication and collaboration, and expand the possibilities for creative expression. The advent of the internet, for instance, has revolutionized how ideas are shared, discussed, and refined, allowing for rapid and widespread dissemination of information. This, in turn, accelerates the evolution and adaptation of ideas as they encounter diverse perspectives and feedback from a global audience.

Creativity and innovation are fundamental drivers of the evolution of ideas. Creativity involves the generation of new and original ideas, while innovation refers to the practical implementation and application of those ideas. Both processes are essential for pushing the boundaries of existing knowledge and driving progress in various fields. Through creativity, individuals and communities can explore novel connections, challenge established conventions, and propose alternative solutions. Innovation transforms these creative ideas into tangible outcomes, contributing to societal development and change.

Moreover, creativity and innovation often thrive in environments that encourage openness, diversity, and collaboration. When different perspectives and disciplines come together, they can spark innovative ideas and foster interdisciplinary approaches. Collaborative efforts, such as research teams or creative communities, allow for the exchange of knowledge and expertise, fueling the evolution of ideas through collective intelligence.

In conclusion, ideas evolve and adapt over time through a complex interplay with cultural, social, and technological changes. The role of creativity and innovation is instrumental in driving this evolution, as they generate innovative ideas and propel their practical implementation. By understanding and appreciating these dynamics, we can better appreciate how ideas shape our world and contribute to its ongoing transformation.

# CHAPTER 3
# THE INFLUENCE OF IDEAS ON SOCIETY

I deas have a profound influence on society and play a critical role in shaping its development. Throughout history, transformative ideas have sparked revolutions, social movements, scientific advancements, and cultural shifts.

## CULTURAL AND SOCIAL CHANGE

Ideas have the power to challenge existing norms, beliefs, and values, leading to cultural and social change. They can originate from various sources, including individuals, intellectual movements, literature, art, science, and technology. When influential ideas take hold and resonate with people, they can catalyze shifts in beliefs, values, behaviors, and institutions, ultimately leading to cultural and social transformation.

Ideas have the power to shape the beliefs and values of individuals and communities. They can challenge existing norms, traditions, and ideologies and introduce new perspectives. For example, during the Enlightenment period in Europe, ideas promoting reason, individualism, and the importance of human rights contributed to the emergence of democratic societies.

Ideas that question or challenge existing power structures can be catalysts for social change. Movements like feminism, civil rights, and LGBTQ+ rights have been fueled by ideas that challenge traditional notions of power, equality, and social justice.

Ideas can inspire social movements by providing a vision for change and mobilizing individuals to act collectively. Think of the ideas of freedom, equality, and justice that influenced movements like the American Civil Rights Movement, the anti-apartheid movement in South Africa, or the Arab Spring uprisings.

Ideas have the potential to transform institutions by challenging established practices and advocating for new ways of organizing society. For example, the idea of inclusive education has led to reforms in educational systems to provide equal opportunities for all students, regardless of their background.

Ideas and innovation are closely linked, and breakthrough ideas have driven technological advancements that have transformed society. The ideas behind the Industrial Revolution, for instance, led to significant changes in manufacturing, transportation, and communication, revolutionizing the way people lived and worked.

Ideas can facilitate cultural exchange and cross-pollination of perspectives. Through art, literature, music, and other forms of cultural expression, ideas can transcend borders and foster understanding, tolerance, and appreciation of diverse cultures.

It is important to note that the influence of ideas on society is complex and multifaceted. Ideas interact with a variety of factors, including historical context, socioeconomic conditions, political systems, and individual agency. Additionally, the dissemination of ideas and their impact can be influenced by media, education, and the power dynamics within a society.

Ideas are powerful forces that shape society and drive cultural and social change. They challenge existing beliefs, inspire movements, transform institutions, foster technological advancements, and promote cultural exchange. Understanding the influence of ideas can help us recognize and analyze the dynamics of social change and contribute to shaping a more inclusive and progressive society.

## SCIENTIFIC AND TECHNOLOGICAL PROGRESS

Scientific ideas drive progress and innovation. Revolutionary scientific theories and discoveries have transformed our understanding of the world and led to advancements in various fields, such as medicine, technology, and communication. Ideas like quantum mechanics, the theory of evolution, and the concept of relativity have shaped the course of scientific and technological development.

Scientific and technological progress has had a profound influence on society, shaping the way we live, work, and interact with one another. However, it's important to note that scientific and technological progress is not solely driven by ideas but also by a range of factors, including economic, political, and cultural dynamics. Nonetheless, ideas play a significant role in guiding scientific and technological progress and their subsequent impact on society.

Revolutionary scientific ideas and technological breakthroughs have led to paradigm shifts, challenging existing beliefs and transforming entire fields. For example, the Copernican revolution in astronomy, driven by the idea of a heliocentric solar system, fundamentally changed our understanding of the universe and our place within it.

Scientific ideas inspire researchers and innovators to solve complex problems and develop new technologies. Ideas serve as a starting point for scientific inquiry, leading to the development of practical applications that address societal needs. For instance, the idea of harnessing electricity led to the invention of various electrical devices, revolutionizing industries, and improving people's quality of life.

Ideas facilitate the sharing of knowledge and collaboration among scientists, technologists, and society at large. The dissemination of ideas through scientific publications, conferences, and online platforms enables the exchange of information and fosters collaboration, accelerating scientific and technological progress. This interconnectedness has amplified the impact of ideas on society.

Ideas also shape society's ethical framework and guide the responsible development and use of scientific and technological advancements. Ethical discussions surrounding topics like genetic engineering, artificial intelligence, and privacy reflect society's efforts to grapple with the potential consequences and implications of these ideas. As a result, ideas can influence the development of regulations, policies, and social norms to ensure responsible and beneficial applications of scientific and technological progress.

Scientific and technological progress can challenge existing cultural norms and societal values, leading to shifts in perception and behavior. For instance, the idea of gender equality has influenced the advancement of women in

STEM fields, challenging traditional gender roles and fostering a more inclusive scientific and technological community.

Ideas arising from scientific and technological progress drive education and public engagement initiatives. Science communication efforts, museums, science festivals, and popular media play a vital role in disseminating ideas to the public, fostering scientific literacy, and promoting informed decision-making in society.

It's important to recognize that the impact of ideas on society through scientific and technological progress is not always linear or predictable. The interplay of various factors, including economic considerations, cultural contexts, and political dynamics, can shape the translation of ideas into tangible societal outcomes. Nevertheless, ideas are a driving force behind scientific and technological progress, influencing the trajectory of society in significant ways.

## POLITICAL AND IDEOLOGICAL MOVEMENTS

Ideas often fuel political and ideological movements that aim to bring about societal change. Concepts such as democracy, communism, human rights, feminism, and environmentalism have mobilized people, challenged existing power structures, and led to significant shifts in political systems and policies.

Political and ideological movements have a significant influence on society through the dissemination and promotion of ideas. Ideas shape the beliefs, values, and behaviors of individuals, and when embraced collectively, they can lead to profound social and cultural changes. The impact of ideas on society can be seen in various aspects, including politics, social norms, economics, and even technological advancements.

Political movements are often founded on specific ideologies and ideas about how society should be organized and governed. For example, the ideas of democracy, equality, and individual rights have been central to the development of liberal democratic systems. Movements advocating for these ideas, such as the Enlightenment and the American and French Revolutions, have played crucial roles in shaping political systems and institutions worldwide.

Ideological movements can challenge and transform existing social norms and values. For instance, the civil rights movement in the United States during the mid-20th century fought against racial segregation and discrimination, ultimately leading to significant changes in social attitudes and legislation. Similarly, feminist movements have challenged traditional gender roles and norms, resulting in greater gender equality and expanded opportunities for women.

Ideas about economic organization, such as capitalism, socialism, or communism, have had a profound impact on societies. Movements advocating for these different economic ideologies have shaped economic policies, labor rights, wealth distribution, and social welfare systems. The rise of neoliberalism in the late 20th century, for example, led to a global shift toward market-oriented policies, deregulation, and privatization.

Ideological movements can also influence technological advancements and innovation. Movements focused on environmentalism and sustainability, for instance, have contributed to the adoption of renewable energy sources, the development of eco-friendly technologies, and the promotion of conservation efforts. Similarly, movements advocating for open-source software and information freedom have influenced the development of the digital landscape and the concept of collaborative knowledge sharing.

Political and ideological movements often inspire cultural and artistic expressions that reflect their ideas and values. Art, literature, music, and cinema have been powerful mediums for conveying and challenging societal norms, political systems, and prevailing ideologies. Movements such as the Harlem Renaissance, the Beat Generation, or the Punk movement have not only influenced artistic trends but also stimulated broader social and cultural change.

It is important to note that the impact of ideas on society is complex and multifaceted. Ideas can inspire positive social change, but they can also be used to justify discrimination, oppression, or divisive ideologies. Furthermore, societal change is often the result of a dynamic interplay between multiple ideas, movements, and historical circumstances. Nonetheless, political, and ideological movements remain crucial in shaping the ideas that shape our society.

## ECONOMIC SYSTEMS AND POLICIES

Economic ideas shape the functioning of societies. For instance, the concept of capitalism, with its emphasis on private property, market competition, and free enterprise, has influenced the economic systems of many countries. Similarly, socialist ideas advocate for collective ownership and distribution of resources, influencing economic policies in various regions.

Ideas play a significant role in shaping society, and economic systems and policies are no exception. The influence of ideas on society through economic systems and policies can be observed in various ways.

Economic systems are shaped by a set of ideas and principles that guide their functioning. For example, capitalism, socialism, and communism are all economic systems that are influenced by different ideas about the role of the state, private property, and market forces. The prevailing ideas about economic organization and resource allocation significantly impact the structure, functioning, and outcomes of the economic system.

Economic policies are formulated based on ideas and theories about how the economy works and how it can be managed to achieve desired outcomes. Different schools

45

of thought, such as Keynesian economics, monetarism, or supply-side economics, provide different perspectives on the role of government, monetary policy, fiscal policy, and regulation. These ideas shape the formulation of policies that aim to address issues such as unemployment, inflation, income inequality, and economic growth.

Economic systems and policies reflect the values and priorities of a society. Ideas about social justice, equality, individual freedom, and sustainability influence the design and implementation of economic systems and policies. For example, ideas about income redistribution and social welfare may lead to policies such as progressive taxation or social safety nets, aimed at reducing inequality and providing a basic standard of living for all citizens.

Ideas can also influence economic systems and policies by fostering innovation and entrepreneurship. Policies that promote intellectual property rights, provide incentives for research and development, or support entrepreneurship are based on the idea that innovation drives economic growth and prosperity. These policies can shape the direction and pace of technological advancements and influence the overall economic performance of a society.

Ideas about economic systems and policies are not solely determined by experts or policymakers. Public opinion and political discourse also play a crucial role in shaping economic systems and policies. Ideas that gain popular support or are championed by influential groups can influence the direction of economic policies. Public sentiment and the acceptance or rejection of certain ideas can lead to policy shifts or reforms.

It is important to note that the relationship between ideas, economic systems, and policies is complex and dynamic. Ideas can evolve over time, and their influence on economic systems and policies can vary across different societies and historical periods. Additionally, economic systems and policies can, in turn, influence and shape the prevailing ideas in a society, creating a feedback loop of mutual influence.

## MORAL AND ETHICAL FRAMEWORKS

Ideas about morality and ethics significantly impact societal values and behaviors. Concepts like justice, equality, liberty, and human rights shape the ethical frameworks upon which societies are built. Changing ideas about morality can lead to shifts in societal attitudes towards issues such as gender equality, LGBTQ+ rights, and racial justice. These frameworks provide a set of principles, values, and guidelines that individuals and communities use to evaluate the moral worth and ethical implications of ideas, actions, and decisions. The interaction between ideas and moral and ethical frameworks can have profound effects on society in several ways.

Moral and ethical frameworks provide a basis for evaluating the moral worth of different ideas. They help individuals and communities determine whether an idea aligns with their ethical values, such as fairness, justice, compassion, and human rights. For example, an idea that promotes equality and social justice may be widely accepted and supported within a framework that values these principles, while an idea that promotes discrimination or harm may face opposition.

Moral and ethical frameworks influence public opinion by providing a lens through which people interpret and evaluate ideas. Individuals tend to align themselves with frameworks that resonate with their core values and beliefs. When ideas align with their moral and ethical frameworks, they are more likely to be embraced and promoted by individuals and communities. Conversely, ideas that contradict or challenge prevailing moral and ethical frameworks may face resistance or skepticism.

Moral and ethical frameworks inform the development of policies and legislation within societies. They help policymakers and legislators determine what is morally acceptable and ethically justifiable. Ideas that align with prevailing moral and ethical frameworks are more likely to be incorporated into policy and legislation, while ideas that clash with these frameworks may encounter barriers or be rejected altogether.

Moral and ethical frameworks shape social norms and behavior by providing guidance on what is considered morally right or wrong and ethically acceptable or unacceptable. When ideas are consistent with prevailing frameworks, they can contribute to the establishment of new social norms and behaviors. Over time, these ideas can influence societal attitudes and practices. For instance, the acceptance of ideas promoting environmental sustainability has led to increased emphasis on recycling and renewable energy sources.

Ideas that challenge prevailing moral and ethical frameworks can have a transformative impact on society. They can initiate debates, discussions, and social movements aimed at reevaluating existing norms and values. Historically, many social and political changes have occurred through the introduction of new ideas that challenge established moral and ethical frameworks, such as the civil rights movement or the push for gender equality.

It is important to note that moral and ethical frameworks can vary across cultures, religions, and philosophical traditions. Different frameworks may prioritize different values and principles, leading to varying interpretations and evaluations of ideas. Additionally, moral, and ethical frameworks are not fixed and can evolve over time in response to socictal changes and new ideas.

## ARTISTIC AND CULTURAL EXPRESSIONS

Ideas and artistic movements influence the cultural landscape of societies. Artistic ideas can spark conversations, challenge the status quo, and contribute to cultural evolution. Ideas conveyed through various art forms, such as visual arts, music, literature, film, theater, and dance, have the power to challenge established norms, provoke thought, inspire change, and create social movements.

Artistic and cultural expressions often reflect the values, beliefs, and concerns of a society or a particular group within it. They provide a platform for artists to explore and communicate their perspectives on social, political, and cultural issues. By capturing the zeitgeist of their time, artists can foster a sense of identity, empathy, and solidarity within a community.

Art has historically played a vital role in challenging established norms and questioning authority. Through their work, artists can provoke critical thinking and encourage societal introspection. Artistic expressions can challenge social injustices, expose inequalities, and shed light on marginalized voices and experiences. By pushing boundaries and questioning prevailing ideas, artists contribute to the progress and evolution of society.

Artistic and cultural expressions have the capacity to foster empathy and understanding by presenting diverse perspectives and experiences. By representing different cultures, identities, and lived realities, art can bridge gaps between people and foster dialogue. It can challenge stereotypes, promote inclusivity, and encourage viewers or participants to see the world from new and unfamiliar angles.

Art has the power to inspire social movements and bring about tangible change. Throughout history, artists have used their work as a medium for activism and advocacy, addressing issues such as civil rights, gender equality, environmental conservation, and more. Artistic expressions can galvanize public sentiment, raise awareness, and mobilize communities to act.

Artistic and cultural expressions shape the narratives and collective memory of a society. They contribute to the construction of cultural identities and help define what is considered significant or valuable. Through art, cultural practices, traditions, and stories are passed down from generation to generation, preserving and shaping the cultural heritage of a community.

Artistic and cultural expressions encourage imagination, innovation, and creativity. They provide spaces for experimentation, free thinking, and the exploration of new ideas. By challenging conventional thinking and pushing the boundaries of what is possible, art inspires individuals to think beyond the limitations imposed by society, fostering a climate of innovation and progress.

Artistic and cultural expressions have a profound influence on society by conveying ideas, challenging norms, fostering empathy, inspiring change, shaping narratives, and stimulating creativity. They serve as catalysts for social transformation, helping to shape the values, beliefs, and aspirations of communities, and contributing to the overall development and progress of society.

The influence of ideas on society can be complex and multifaceted. Factors such as historical context, social dynamics, and individual agency also play a role in how ideas are adopted and implemented. Nonetheless, ideas have proven to be powerful catalysts for change throughout history, shaping the course of societies in profound ways.

The transformative power of ideas on societal structures and norms is a fascinating subject of study. Ideas have the potential to shape political systems, economies, and social movements by challenging existing beliefs, introducing new paradigms, and inspiring collective action. Throughout history, influential thinkers and their ideas have played a crucial role in shaping the world we live in today.

## 1. Political Systems:

Ideas can reshape political systems by challenging traditional power structures and advocating for new forms of governance. For example, the Enlightenment philosophers, such as John Locke and Montesquieu, promoted the ideas of individual rights, separation of powers, and social contract. These concepts laid the foundation for modern democracies and influenced the development of political systems worldwide. Similarly, Karl Marx's ideas on communism and class struggle sparked revolutionary movements and shaped political systems in various countries.

## 2. Economies:

Ideas also have a profound impact on economic systems. Prominent economists like Adam Smith and his idea of free markets and the invisible hand have significantly influenced capitalist economies. Smith's concept of self-interest driving economic growth and the idea of limited government intervention shaped the development of market-oriented systems. On the other hand, the ideas of John Maynard Keynes regarding government intervention and fiscal policies during times of economic downturn have had a transformative effect on modern welfare states.

## 3. Social Movements:

Ideas are often at the core of social movements that challenge prevailing norms and advocate for change. For instance, the Civil Rights Movement in the United States was fueled by the ideas of equality, justice, and nonviolent resistance propagated by influential figures like Martin Luther King Jr. These ideas not only transformed societal attitudes but also led to significant legislative changes and advancements in civil rights. Similarly, feminist movements have been driven by ideas of gender equality, challenging traditional gender roles, and promoting women's rights.

## 4. Influential Thinkers:

The ideas put forth by influential thinkers throughout history have had a lasting impact on society. Thinkers like Plato, Aristotle, Thomas Hobbes, and John Stuart Mill have shaped political philosophy and our understanding of governance. Their ideas on justice, liberty, and the role of the state continue to inform political debates. In the realm of economics, figures like Friedrich Hayek, Milton Friedman, and Amartya Sen have made significant contributions through their ideas on free markets, neoliberalism, and development economics, respectively.

Moreover, the advent of the internet and globalization has amplified the dissemination and influence of ideas. Online platforms have enabled the rapid spread of ideas, allowing social movements to mobilize and gain momentum quickly. The democratization of knowledge has empowered individuals to challenge existing power structures and norms, as seen in recent social and political movements worldwide.

In conclusion, ideas have a transformative power over societal structures and norms. They shape political systems, economies, and social movements by challenging established beliefs, introducing new perspectives, and inspiring collective action. Influential thinkers and their ideas have played a crucial role in shaping the world we live in, leaving a lasting impact on how we govern ourselves, conduct economic affairs, and strive for social change.

CHAPTER 4

# IDEAS THAT CHANGED THE WORLD

T here have been numerous ideas throughout history that have had a profound impact on the world. Here are some ideas that have shaped the course of human civilization.

## DEMOCRACY

Democracy is a form of government that has had a profound impact on the world throughout history. Several key ideas and principles associated with democracy have shaped societies, challenged traditional power structures, and fostered the growth of individual freedoms and human rights.

The concept of popular sovereignty asserts that the ultimate source of political power resides with the people. This idea challenged the notion of divine right and absolute monarchy, paving the way for governments that derive their legitimacy from the consent of the governed.

Democracy emphasizes the rule of law, which means that laws are supreme and apply equally to all citizens, including those in positions of power. This principle ensures that no one is above the law and protects individual rights and liberties.

The idea of universal suffrage, or the right of all adult citizens to vote, has been a transformative democratic principle. The expansion of suffrage to previously marginalized groups, such as women and racial minorities, has led to more inclusive and representative governments.

The concept of separating powers into distinct branches— legislative, executive, and judicial—establishes a system of checks and balances. This division of power prevents any single entity from becoming too dominant and helps safeguard against tyranny.

Democracy promotes the freedom of speech and expression,

recognizing the importance of allowing individuals to voice their opinions, criticize the government, and participate in public discourse without fear of repression. This idea has been crucial in fostering open societies and encouraging diverse viewpoints.

Democracy values a free and independent press as a cornerstone of a well-informed citizenry. A robust press acts as a watchdog, holding governments accountable and facilitating the dissemination of information necessary for an engaged electorate.

Democracy recognizes and protects fundamental human rights, including but not limited to freedom of assembly, freedom of religion, and the right to due process. The idea that all individuals possess inherent rights that must be respected has influenced the development of international human rights frameworks.

Peaceful transfer of power is a defining characteristic of democratic systems. This idea contrasts with authoritarian regimes, where transitions often involve violence or coercion. The peaceful transfer of power allows for stability, continuity, and a means for citizens to effect change through elections.

These ideas of democracy have had a profound impact on societies worldwide, fostering greater political participation, promoting human rights, and challenging oppressive systems. While democratic ideals continue to evolve and face challenges, they have undeniably shaped the modern world and inspired movements for freedom and equality.

# SCIENTIFIC METHOD

The scientific method, developed during the Scientific Revolution, transformed the way we acquire knowledge. It emphasizes empirical evidence, experimentation, and critical thinking, leading to groundbreaking discoveries and advancements in various fields. It has played a pivotal role in advancing our understanding of the world and has led to numerous groundbreaking discoveries and innovations.

The scientific method emphasizes the importance of making objective observations of the natural world. This idea revolutionized our understanding of the physical and biological phenomena around us, leading to discoveries such as gravity, the laws of motion, and the classification of species.

The method encourages the formulation of testable hypotheses to explain natural phenomena. This approach has led to significant breakthroughs, such as the theory of evolution by natural selection, the discovery of DNA's structure, and the identification of the Higgs boson particle.

It promotes the use of controlled experiments to investigate causal relationships between variables. This methodology has been instrumental in fields like medicine, allowing the development of effective treatments and vaccines, as well as in physics and chemistry, enabling the discovery of new materials and reactions.

The scientific method involves subjecting research to rigorous peer review by experts in the field. This process ensures that scientific findings meet high standards of quality, accuracy, and validity. Peer review has been crucial in maintaining scientific integrity and preventing the dissemination of false or misleading information.

It emphasizes the importance of quantifying and measuring phenomena to obtain reliable data. This approach has led to the development of precise measurements, such as the speed of light, the size of atoms, and the temperature scales. Accurate measurements have enabled advancements in fields ranging from astronomy to nanotechnology.

The method is an iterative process that involves continuous refinement and revision of theories and models based on new evidence. This approach has led to paradigm shifts in various disciplines, such as the transition from the geocentric to the heliocentric model of the solar system and the development of quantum mechanics.

The scientific method emphasizes the importance of reproducibility, where experiments and findings can be independently verified by other researchers. This principle ensures that scientific knowledge is reliable and robust, allowing for the validation of results and the identification of potential errors or biases.

These ideas of the scientific method have revolutionized our understanding of the natural world and have paved the way for countless scientific discoveries and technological advancements that have shaped our modern society.

## INDUSTRIAL REVOLUTION

The Industrial Revolution was a period of profound transformation in the late 18th and early 19th centuries that had a significant impact on the world. It brought about numerous ideas and innovations that revolutionized various aspects of society, economy, and technology.

One of the fundamental ideas of the Industrial Revolution was the shift from manual labor to machine-based production. The invention of machines such as the steam engine and textile machinery revolutionized manufacturing processes, increasing productivity and efficiency.

The concept of mass production emerged during the Industrial Revolution. Factories introduced assembly lines and standardized processes, allowing goods to be produced on a large scale. This led to increased availability of affordable products and the rise of consumer culture.

The Industrial Revolution led to a massive migration of people from rural areas to urban centers. The growth of factories and industries concentrated in cities, creating opportunities for employment, and contributing to the development of urban infrastructure.

The idea of dividing complex tasks into simpler, specialized tasks emerged during the Industrial Revolution. This division of labor increased efficiency, as workers could focus on specific tasks, leading to increased productivity and the growth of industries.

The Industrial Revolution fostered the growth of capitalism, with entrepreneurs investing in industries and seeking profits. This shift in economic systems encouraged innovation, competition, and the accumulation of wealth, transforming the economic landscape.

The Industrial Revolution saw significant technological advancements in various fields. Alongside the steam engine, innovations such as the spinning jenny, power loom, telegraph, and railway systems transformed communication, transportation, and manufacturing, paving the way for further developments.

The concentration of factories and industries in urban centers resulted in the creation of industrial cities. These cities became hubs of economic activity, attracting workers and fostering the development of infrastructure, trade networks, and cultural institutions.

The Industrial Revolution also sparked debates and

movements for social and labor reforms. Workers' rights, such as the right to fair wages, safe working conditions, and shorter work hours, became significant issues, leading to the formation of labor unions and the push for legislative changes.

The Industrial Revolution facilitated the globalization of trade and the expansion of colonial empires. It led to the increased interconnectivity between nations, the exchange of goods and ideas across borders, and the exploitation of resources in colonies to fuel industrial production.

While the Industrial Revolution brought about numerous advancements, it also had significant environmental consequences. The increased use of fossil fuels, deforestation, and pollution contributed to long-term environmental challenges that we continue to face today.

These are just a few of the many ideas and changes that emerged during the Industrial Revolution. Together, they transformed societies, economies, and technologies, shaping the modern world as we know it.

## THEORY OF EVOLUTION

Charles Darwin's theory of evolution by natural selection introduced the idea that species evolve over time, challenging religious and philosophical beliefs about the origins of life. This theory has had far-reaching implications in biology, genetics, and our understanding of the natural world.

Darwin proposed that all species, including humans, share a common ancestor. This idea challenged the prevailing notion of a static and unchanging world and provided a framework for understanding the diversity of life on Earth.

He proposed that species evolve through a process called natural selection, where individuals with advantageous traits are more likely to survive and reproduce, passing those traits on to future generations. This concept of gradual change over time has transformed our understanding of how species adapt and evolve.

Natural selection is the central mechanism of evolution. It acts on heritable variations within a population, favoring traits that increase an organism's fitness for its environment. Natural selection has far-reaching implications, explaining the origin of complex adaptations and the diversity of life forms.

The theory of evolution emphasizes the concept of adaptation, where organisms become better suited to their environment over time. This idea has helped us understand the incredible diversity and specialization seen in living organisms.

The theory explains how new species arise. Over time, populations can become reproductively isolated from one another, leading to the development of distinct species. This concept has transformed our understanding of the origin and diversity of life forms on Earth.

The theory of evolution is supported by a vast amount of fossil evidence, which provides a record of past life forms and their changes over time. Fossils have allowed scientists to reconstruct the history of life on Earth and provide concrete evidence for the process of evolution.

The theory of evolution has greatly influenced the field of molecular biology and genetics. By studying DNA and genetic variation, scientists have been able to trace evolutionary relationships, identify common ancestors, and understand the mechanisms behind evolutionary change.

Evolutionary principles have important implications for medicine and our understanding of diseases. The theory of evolution helps us understand the emergence and spread of antibiotic resistance, the evolution of pathogens, and the genetic basis of human diseases.

The theory of evolution provides a foundation for understanding biodiversity and has significant implications for conservation efforts. By recognizing the interconnectedness of species and their evolutionary histories, scientists can better understand the importance of preserving ecosystems and preventing species extinctions.

In human evolution, the theory of evolution has had a transformative impact on our understanding of human origins and our place in the natural world. It has shed light on our shared ancestry with other primates and the gradual development of distinct human traits over time.

These ideas have revolutionized our understanding of the natural world and continue to shape scientific research and various disciplines, from biology and anthropology to medicine and conservation. The theory of evolution stands as one of the most influential scientific theories ever proposed.

## UNIVERSAL HUMAN RIGHTS

The concept of universal human rights emerged as a response to widespread injustices and inequalities. They are fundamental principles that protect the dignity, equality, and freedoms of all individuals, regardless of their race, religion, gender, nationality, or any other characteristic. It asserts that all individuals are entitled to certain fundamental rights and freedoms, regardless of their nationality, ethnicity, gender, or other characteristics.

Universal Declaration of Human Rights (UDHR) which was adopted by the United Nations General Assembly in 1948, is a landmark document that sets out a broad range of civil, political, economic, social, and cultural rights. It serves as the foundation for the modern concept of human rights and has been instrumental in shaping national and international laws and policies.

The principle of equality asserts that all individuals are born free and equal in dignity and rights. This idea has challenged discriminatory practices, such as racial segregation, apartheid, and gender inequality, and has contributed to significant social and legal changes worldwide.

The right to freedom of expression is a cornerstone of democracy and has played a crucial role in advocating for social justice, promoting accountability, and challenging oppressive regimes. It enables individuals to voice their opinions, criticize governments, and advance social progress.

The movement to abolish slavery was a turning point in human history. The idea that every person has the right to be free from forced labor and servitude challenged the long-standing institution of slavery and led to its eventual eradication in most parts of the world.

The recognition and promotion of women's rights as human rights have transformed societies globally. Ideas advocating for gender equality, such as the right to vote, access to education, and the elimination of discrimination and violence against women, have brought about significant advancements in women's empowerment and gender equality.

The idea that education is a fundamental right has been instrumental in expanding access to education and promoting literacy worldwide. Education empowers individuals, fosters economic development, and enhances social mobility, contributing to the overall well-being of communities and nations.

The concept of the right to privacy has become increasingly important in the digital age. It recognizes individuals' right to protect their personal information, maintain confidentiality, and be free from unwarranted surveillance or intrusion.

The recognition of the rights of lesbian, gay, bisexual, transgender, and queer (LGBTQ+) individuals has challenged discrimination and led to advancements in areas such as decriminalization of homosexuality, marriage equality, and protection against discrimination based on sexual orientation and gender identity.

The acknowledgment and protection of the rights of indigenous peoples have aimed to rectify historical injustices and promote their self-determination, cultural preservation, land rights, and participation in decision-making processes.

These ideas have shaped international human rights law, influenced national legislation, inspired social movements, and changed societal norms, contributing to a more just and inclusive world. While progress is ongoing, the advocacy for universal human rights continues to be a driving force for positive change.

## INTERNET AND WORLD WIDE WEB

The invention of the internet and the subsequent development of the World Wide Web revolutionized communication and information sharing on a global scale. It has transformed various aspects of life, including education, commerce, and social interactions.

With regards to global communication, the Internet allows people from all over the world to connect and communicate in real-time. Email, instant messaging, social media platforms, and video conferencing have made it easier for individuals, businesses, and communities to interact and collaborate across borders.

The World Wide Web provides unprecedented access to information. Online search engines, such as Google, enable users to find information on virtually any topic within seconds. This accessibility has democratized knowledge and empowered individuals to learn, explore, and make informed decisions.

The rise of the Internet has revolutionized the way we buy and sell goods and services. E-commerce platforms, like Amazon and Alibaba, have transformed traditional retail models, offering convenience, global reach, and access to a wide variety of products. Online shopping has become an integral part of our daily lives.

Social media platforms like Facebook, Twitter, Instagram, and LinkedIn have redefined the way we connect and interact with others. They allow individuals to share their thoughts, experiences, and media, fostering new forms of communication, community-building, and even social activism.

The Internet has opened new opportunities for education and learning. Online courses, webinars, and educational platforms like Coursera and Khan Academy have made education more accessible to people worldwide, regardless of their location or socioeconomic background.

Platforms like Wikipedia and open-source communities have harnessed the power of collective intelligence, enabled collaborative creation and sharing of knowledge. These initiatives have resulted in vast repositories of information that are freely accessible to all.

The Internet has transformed the entertainment industry. Streaming services like Netflix and Spotify have disrupted traditional media consumption patterns, offering on-demand access to movies, TV shows, music, and podcasts. Online gaming has also become a multi-billion-dollar industry, connecting players globally.

The Internet has provided a platform for marginalized voices, enabling individuals and communities to express themselves, share their stories, and advocate for social change. Online activism and social movements have gained momentum through hashtags, viral campaigns, and crowdfunding platforms.

The advent of cloud computing has revolutionized the way data is stored, accessed, and processed. Cloud-based services, like Dropbox and Google Drive, offer convenient and scalable storage solutions, enabling individuals and businesses to access their files from anywhere and collaborate seamlessly.

The Internet of Things (IoT) refers to the network of interconnected devices that communicate and share data with each other over the Internet. IoT has the potential to transform various sectors, including healthcare, transportation, and smart homes, by creating more efficient and interconnected systems.

These internet and world wide web ideas, among others, have transformed the world and continue to shape our lives in numerous ways, ushering in an era of connectivity, convenience, and unprecedented access to information and opportunities.

## THEORY OF RELATIVITY

The theory of relativity, developed by Albert Einstein in the early 20th century, revolutionized our understanding of space, time, and gravity. It introduced the concept that the laws of physics are the same for all observers and led to advancements in cosmology, astrophysics, and technology.

Einstein's theory of relativity introduced the concept of space and time being interconnected, forming a four-dimensional framework called space-time. This idea fundamentally changed our understanding of the nature of space and time and provided a new mathematical framework for describing the behavior of objects in the universe.

According to the theory of relativity, the concept of simultaneity is relative to the observer's frame of reference. Events that are simultaneous for one observer may not be simultaneous for another observer moving relative to the first. This understanding of the relativity of simultaneity challenged the classical notion of absolute time and led to a profound shift in our understanding of time itself.

One of the most famous aspects of the theory of relativity is the phenomenon of time dilation. According to this idea, time can appear to run slower or faster depending on the relative motion between two observers. This has been confirmed through numerous experiments and has practical applications in technologies such as GPS, where precise timing is crucial.

Einstein's famous equation $E=mc^2$ expresses the mass-energy equivalence, stating that mass can be converted into energy and vice versa. This revolutionary concept laid the foundation for the development of nuclear energy and the understanding of the tremendous amounts of energy released in processes such as nuclear fission and fusion.

General relativity predicts that massive objects can bend the path of light passing near them, creating a gravitational lensing effect. This prediction has been observed and verified, and it has provided astronomers with a powerful tool for studying distant galaxies and uncovering the presence of dark matter. General relativity also predicted the existence of black holes, objects with such strong gravitational pull that nothing, not even light, can escape their gravitational field. The understanding and study of black holes have revolutionized our understanding of the universe, leading to new insights into the nature of space, time, and gravity.

Einstein's theory of general relativity forms the basis of modern cosmology, the study of the origin, evolution, and structure of the universe. It provided a framework for understanding the expansion of the universe and led to the development of the Big Bang theory, which explains the origin of the universe.

These are just a few examples of how the theory of relativity has changed our world. Einstein's ideas have had profound implications in physics, astronomy, technology, and our overall understanding of the universe. They continue to inspire scientific research and shape our view of the cosmos.

## FEMINISM

The feminist movement, spanning different waves throughout history, advocated for gender equality, and challenged traditional gender roles and discrimination. One of the core ideas of feminism is the belief in equal rights, opportunities, and treatment for people of all genders. This concept has challenged the historically entrenched notion of gender roles and expectations, promoting the idea that everyone should have the same rights and opportunities, regardless of their gender.

The feminist movement played a crucial role in the fight for women's suffrage, which led to women gaining the right to vote in many countries around the world. This monumental achievement marked a significant milestone in the progress towards gender equality and paved the way for women's participation in politics and decision-making processes.

Feminism has fought for reproductive rights, including access to contraception and safe, legal abortion. These efforts aimed to give women control over their bodies and reproductive choices, empowering them to make decisions about their own health, family planning, and careers.

Intersectional feminism recognizes that gender intersects with other social identities, such as race, class, sexuality, and disability, leading to unique experiences and forms of discrimination. This concept highlights the importance of addressing the overlapping systems of oppression and advocating for the rights and needs of marginalized women.

The persistent gender pay gap has been a key focus of feminist activism. Advocates have worked to raise awareness about the unequal wages between men and women performing the same work, pushing for fair pay practices and policies to address this issue.

Feminism has played a vital role in raising awareness about sexual harassment and violence against women. The #MeToo movement, for example, shed light on the prevalence of sexual misconduct and sparked a global conversation about consent, power dynamics, and the need for accountability.

Feminism has challenged narrow beauty standards and promoted body positivity, embracing diverse body types, and rejecting unrealistic ideals. This movement has aimed to foster self-acceptance, promote healthy body image, and challenge the objectification of women's bodies in media and society.

Feminism has advocated for policies and cultural shifts to support work-life balance for both men and women. This includes initiatives like parental leave, flexible working arrangements, and shared caregiving responsibilities, allowing individuals to fulfill their professional aspirations while also maintaining their personal lives.

## GREEN REVOLUTION

The Green Revolution refers to a series of agricultural innovations and practices that occurred in the mid-20th century, primarily from the 1940s to the 1970s. These revolutionary ideas and advancements in agriculture led to significant increases in crop yields and transformed agricultural practices worldwide. Here are some key ideas and technologies associated with the Green Revolution:

The development of high-yielding crop varieties, such as

wheat and rice, was a breakthrough. Scientists selectively bred varieties that had increased resistance to diseases, pests, and environmental stresses while producing higher yields.

The use of hybrid seeds, which resulted from crossbreeding different varieties of plants, led to improved crop productivity. Hybrid seeds had better traits like higher yields, disease resistance, and uniformity.

The Green Revolution promoted the extensive use of synthetic fertilizers to enhance soil fertility. This enabled crops to receive optimal nutrient levels, leading to increased yields. The development and use of chemical pesticides and herbicides helped control crop pests and weeds effectively, minimizing crop losses and improving productivity.

Efficient irrigation methods, including the use of tube wells, sprinklers, and drip irrigation, allowed farmers to provide adequate water to crops, especially in regions with limited rainfall. The Green Revolution emphasized the adoption of machinery like tractors, threshers, and harvesters, which reduced the dependence on human labor and increased efficiency in farm operations.

Better storage facilities, such as warehouses and silos, were introduced to prevent post-harvest losses. Additionally, improved transportation networks and infrastructure facilitated the efficient distribution of agricultural produce.

The Green Revolution highlighted the importance of scientific research and education in agriculture. It led to the establishment of agricultural universities and research institutes that focused on developing new technologies and training farmers.

To disseminate the latest agricultural practices, extension services were established to provide training and guidance to farmers. Agricultural experts and scientists worked closely with farmers to share knowledge and help them adopt modern techniques.

The innovations of the Green Revolution significantly increased global food production, helping to alleviate hunger and food shortages in many parts of the world.

The ideas and technologies of the Green Revolution transformed agriculture by boosting crop yields, improving food security, and increasing farm incomes. However, it is important to note that the Green Revolution also had some negative consequences, such as environmental impacts, depletion of natural resources, and social inequalities. Today, sustainable agriculture practices aim to build upon the successes of the Green Revolution while addressing these concerns.

## THEORY OF SPECIAL RELATIVITY

The theory of special relativity, formulated by Albert Einstein in 1905, revolutionized our understanding of space, time, and the nature of physical laws. It introduced several groundbreaking ideas that have had a profound impact on science, technology, and our view of the universe.

According to special relativity, the concept of simultaneous events is relative and depends on the observer's frame of reference. This challenged the classical notion of absolute time and introduced the idea that time can be experienced differently by observers in relative motion. The relativity of simultaneity has influenced fields such as physics, philosophy, and even our understanding of causality.

Special relativity revealed that time is not an absolute quantity but is affected by motion. The theory predicts that time appears to slow down for objects moving relative to an observer. This phenomenon, known as time dilation, has been verified experimentally and has practical applications in various areas, such as satellite navigation systems and particle accelerators.

Another consequence of special relativity is the concept of length contraction. As an object moves relative to an observer, its length appears to contract along the direction of motion. This effect has been observed in high-speed particle experiments and has implications for space travel and our understanding of the geometry of the universe.

One of the most famous equations in physics, $E=mc^2$, arises from special relativity. It states that mass and energy are interchangeable, and a small amount of mass can be converted into a large amount of energy. This insight led to the development of nuclear energy and fundamentally changed our understanding of the relationship between matter and energy.

Special relativity introduced a new formula for momentum that accounts for the effects of high speeds. It showed that the momentum of an object increases as it approaches the speed of light. This discovery has influenced fields such as particle physics and has implications for space travel and the behavior of high-energy particles.

Special relativity unified electricity and magnetism into a single theory known as electromagnetism. It showed that electric and magnetic fields are two aspects of the same phenomenon and depend on the relative motion of the observer. This understanding laid the foundation for the development of modern physics and led to advances in technology, including the development of electronics and wireless communication.

While special relativity deals with objects moving in the absence of gravity, it paved the way for Einstein's later theory of general relativity, which includes the effects of gravity. General relativity revolutionized our understanding of gravity, describing it as the curvature of spacetime caused by the presence of mass and energy. This theory has been crucial in explaining phenomena such as black holes, the expansion of the universe, and gravitational waves.

These ideas have had a lasting influence on human civilization, shaping our understanding of the world, our social structures, and our cultural expressions. They continue to be relevant and explored in contemporary contexts, driving further progress and innovation. By reflecting on the past and understanding the impact of these ideas, we can gain valuable insights into our present and future trajectory as a civilization.

# CHAPTER 5

# THE POWER OF DISRUPTIVE IDEAS

The power of disruptive ideas lies in their ability to challenge the status quo and bring about meaningful change. Disruptive ideas often involve innovative approaches, technologies, or business models that revolutionize existing industries or create entirely new ones.

Disruptive ideas question traditional practices and challenge existing assumptions. They challenge the "that's how it's always been done" mindset and provide alternative ways of thinking and doing things.

Disruptive ideas have the potential to create new opportunities and markets. By identifying unmet needs or untapped markets, disruptive ideas can introduce products, services, or technologies that fill those gaps, opening new possibilities and driving economic growth.

Disruptive ideas often tackle long-standing challenges or problems that have previously been difficult to address. By thinking creatively and approaching problems from a fresh perspective, disruptive ideas can offer innovative solutions and bring about positive change.

Disruptive ideas can empower individuals and communities by giving them access to resources, knowledge, and tools that were previously unavailable or limited. For example, disruptive technologies like smartphones and the internet have democratized information, communication, and access to markets, enabling people from various backgrounds to participate and contribute.

Disruptive ideas often disrupt existing markets and force established players to adapt or face obsolescence. This competition can drive innovation as companies strive to differentiate themselves and stay relevant. This benefits consumers by offering them a wider range of choices and improved products or services.

Disruptive ideas have the potential to catalyze significant societal progress by addressing pressing issues such as climate change, healthcare accessibility, education, and social inequality. They can introduce breakthrough technologies, alternative energy solutions, sustainable business models, and transformative approaches that contribute to a more sustainable and equitable future.

However, it is important to note that not all disruptive ideas succeed. The execution, timing, market dynamics, and various other factors play a crucial role in determining their success. Nonetheless, the power of disruptive ideas lies in their capacity to challenge the status quo, inspire innovation, and drive positive change across various domains.

Disruptive ideas have the power to challenge established systems and bring about paradigm shifts by introducing innovative concepts, technologies, or approaches that fundamentally transform industries and societies. However, they often face significant resistance to change and hurdles along the way. Let us delve into these aspects and explore examples of disruptive ideas that have revolutionized various domains.

Inertia and Comfort with the Status Quo: Established systems and individuals within them may be resistant to change due to the fear of the unknown or the comfort they find in the current practices.

Financial Interests: Incumbent players, who have invested heavily in existing systems, may resist disruptive ideas that threaten their market share or profitability.

Regulatory and Legal Challenges: Existing regulations and laws can pose barriers to disruptive ideas, especially when they challenge traditional norms or require new frameworks to operate.

## HURDLES FACED BY DISRUPTIVE IDEAS

Skepticism and Criticism: Disruptive ideas are often met with skepticism and criticism from experts and industry leaders, who may doubt their feasibility or long-term sustainability.

Market Adoption Challenges: Convincing customers to embrace innovative ideas and shift away from established solutions can be a significant hurdle, especially if disruptive ideas require changes in behavior or infrastructure.

Resource Constraints: Developing and implementing disruptive ideas may require substantial resources, including financial investment, skilled talent, and infrastructure, posing challenges for startups or organizations with limited means.

## EXAMPLES OF DISRUPTIVE IDEAS

**Uber:** Uber revolutionized the transportation industry by introducing a ride-sharing platform that challenged traditional taxi services. It leveraged mobile technology and a decentralized model, creating a change in basic assumptions in how people access transportation services.

**Airbnb:** By enabling homeowners to rent out their properties to travelers, Airbnb disrupted the hospitality industry. It offered an alternative to traditional hotels and accommodations, empowering individuals and transforming the way people travel.

**Tesla:** Tesla disrupted the automotive industry by introducing electric vehicles (EVs) that demonstrated the feasibility and desirability of sustainable transportation. It challenged the dominance of traditional gasoline-powered cars and paved the way for the widespread adoption of EVs.

**Blockchain:** The invention of blockchain technology, popularized by Bitcoin, challenged the established financial systems by introducing a decentralized and transparent approach to recording and verifying transactions. It has the potential to revolutionize various industries beyond finance, such as supply chain management and healthcare.

These examples highlight how disruptive ideas can overcome resistance and hurdles, driving significant changes in industries and societies. By challenging the status quo, they have brought about paradigm shifts, often leading to improved efficiency, increased accessibility, and novel business models. However, it is important to acknowledge that not all disruptive ideas succeed, and some face insurmountable barriers or fail to gain widespread acceptance.

# CHAPTER 6

# THE ROLE OF IDEAS IN PROBLEM-SOLVING

Ideas play a crucial role in problem-solving as they are the starting point for generating solutions and exploring different possibilities. Ideas are the mental representations or concepts that individuals use to understand and interpret the world around them. They provide the building blocks for problem-solving processes by enabling individuals to conceptualize problems, devise strategies, and generate potential solutions.

Here are some key aspects highlighting the role of ideas in problem-solving:

## PROBLEM IDENTIFICATION

Ideas are instrumental in recognizing and defining problems. They help individuals perceive discrepancies between the current state and the desired state, leading to problem recognition. For example, an idea might spark the realization that a certain process could be more efficient or that a particular challenge needs to be addressed.

Idea Generation: Once a problem is identified, ideas are generated as potential solutions or approaches to address the problem. Idea generation involves creative thinking, brainstorming, and exploring different perspectives. The more diverse and abundant the ideas, the greater the chances of finding effective solutions.

Divergent Thinking: Ideas encourage divergent thinking, which involves generating a wide range of workable solutions or perspectives. This kind of thinking allows for the exploration of multiple options, which can lead to innovative and creative problem-solving approaches. Divergent thinking helps overcome limitations and biases, expanding the range of potential solutions.

## EVALUATION AND SELECTION

Ideas also play a role in evaluating and selecting the most promising solutions. Once a variety of ideas has been generated, they can be critically analyzed based on their feasibility, effectiveness, and alignment with the problem context. This evaluation process helps identify the best ideas to pursue further.

## ITERATIVE PROCESS

Problem-solving is often an iterative process, where ideas and solutions are refined and revised based on feedback and added information. Each iteration builds upon previous ideas, leading to continuous improvement and optimization. Ideas evolve and transform throughout the problem-solving journey.

## OVERCOMING OBSTACLES

Ideas can help overcome obstacles and challenges encountered during problem-solving. They enable individuals to think creatively and produce alternative approaches when faced with roadblocks or setbacks. Ideas provide the flexibility needed to adapt and find new paths towards the desired outcome.

## INNOVATION AND TRANSFORMATION

Ideas are the foundation of innovation and transformative problem-solving. They drive breakthroughs, new discoveries, and novel approaches to complex challenges. By exploring and expanding upon ideas, individuals can push the boundaries of traditional problem-solving methods, leading to significant advancements.

Ideas are fundamental to problem-solving as they shape the entire process from problem identification to solution generation, evaluation, and implementation. They foster creativity, enable flexibility, and drive innovation, allowing individuals to tackle problems from various angles and discover effective solutions.

Ideas play a crucial role in driving innovation and problem-solving. They serve as the starting point for generating innovative approaches, strategies, and solutions to complex challenges. Whether it is a small improvement or a groundbreaking breakthrough, ideas form the foundation upon which problem-solving efforts are built.

One of the keyways in which ideas contribute to finding solutions is by providing alternative perspectives and possibilities. When faced with a complex challenge, a diverse range of ideas allows for a more comprehensive exploration of potential solutions. Each idea brings a unique viewpoint, drawing from different experiences, knowledge, and creativity. This diversity fuels innovation by challenging existing assumptions, expanding the pool of potential solutions, and encouraging out-of-the-box thinking.

Moreover, the iterative nature of problem-solving recognizes that finding the optimal solution often requires multiple cycles of idea generation, testing, and refinement. Each iteration builds upon the insights gained from previous attempts, leading to an incremental improvement or a breakthrough discovery. Ideas function as steppingstones in this process, allowing for continuous exploration, learning, and adaptation.

The power of generating diverse ideas lies in the fact that it increases the chances of finding novel and effective solutions. When confronted with complex challenges, there is rarely a single "right" answer. Instead, a combination of ideas, approaches, and perspectives is often needed to address various aspects of the problem. By fostering a culture that encourages diverse contributions, organizations and teams can tap into a broader range of expertise and experiences, leading to more robust and innovative solutions.

Furthermore, the collaborative aspect of idea generation enhances problem-solving efforts. When individuals with diverse backgrounds and expertise come together to brainstorm and exchange ideas, it creates a synergistic effect. Through constructive dialogue and debate, ideas are refined, combined, and built upon, resulting in more refined and viable solutions.

However, it is important to note that not all ideas will lead to successful solutions. Some ideas may be impractical, unfeasible, or ineffective. Nevertheless, even seemingly "bad" ideas can contribute to the problem-solving process by stimulating new thoughts or triggering innovative thinking in unexpected directions. The iterative nature of problem-solving allows for the exploration of a wide range of ideas, providing opportunities for refinement and course correction.

Ideas are the catalysts that drive innovation and problem-solving. They bring diverse perspectives, fuel iterative processes, and contribute to finding solutions to complex challenges. By encouraging the generation of diverse ideas and embracing an iterative approach, individuals and organizations can tap into the power of collective thinking and unlock new possibilities for innovation and problem-solving.

CHAPTER 7

# HARNESSING THE POWER OF IDEAS

Harnessing the power of ideas is crucial for innovation, problem-solving, and driving progress in various fields.

## CULTIVATE A CREATIVE ENVIRONMENT

Cultivating a creative environment is essential for harnessing the power of ideas and fostering innovation. When individuals feel inspired, supported, and encouraged to think differently, they can generate groundbreaking ideas that can transform organizations and societies.

Foster an atmosphere where everyone feels comfortable expressing their thoughts and opinions. Encourage open and honest dialogue, active listening, and respect for diverse perspectives. This promotes the free flow of ideas and creates a safe space for creativity to thrive.

Recognize the value of diverse backgrounds, experiences, and perspectives. By including individuals with different skill sets, cultures, and ways of thinking, you can tap into a broader range of ideas and innovative solutions. Encourage collaboration among diverse teams to promote creativity and cross-pollination of ideas.

Grant individuals the freedom and autonomy to explore their ideas and take ownership of their work. Avoid micromanagement and excessive control, as it can stifle creativity and limit the potential for innovative thinking. Instead, provide guidance, set clear goals, and trust your team to find creative solutions.

Encourage continuous learning and personal development by providing opportunities for skill-building and knowledge sharing. Support employees in pursuing their passions and interests, both within and outside their immediate roles. Emphasize the importance of experimentation, learning from failures, and embracing a growth mindset.

The physical workspace can significantly impact creativity. Design an environment that is visually appealing, comfortable, and adaptable. Consider flexible workspaces, natural light, and areas for relaxation and brainstorming. Provide tools, resources, and technologies that facilitate idea generation and collaboration.

Encourage individuals to take calculated risks and explore unconventional ideas. Emphasize that failures are learning opportunities and part of the creative process. Celebrate both small and significant successes, encouraging a culture that embraces experimentation and resilience.

Facilitate interactions between different teams, departments, and disciplines. Encourage employees to share their ideas, experiences, and knowledge across silos. Create platforms for cross-functional collaboration, such as brainstorming sessions, innovation workshops, or internal hackathons.

Establish a system that recognizes and rewards creative thinking and innovation. Acknowledge and appreciate individuals who contribute valuable ideas and encourage others to do the same. Offer incentives, such as promotions, bonuses, or special projects, to inspire creativity and maintain motivation.

Leaders play a crucial role in setting the tone for a creative environment. Demonstrate openness to new ideas, actively engage in brainstorming sessions, and support creative initiatives. Encourage risk-taking, provide constructive feedback, and show appreciation for innovative thinking.

Recognize that creativity thrives when individuals have

a healthy work-life balance. Encourage breaks, flexible schedules, and time for personal reflection. Encourage activities outside of work that can inspire creativity, such as hobbies, travel, or exposure to different cultures and art forms.

Remember, cultivating a creative environment is an ongoing process that requires continuous effort and adaptation. By fostering a culture that values and nurtures creativity, organizations can harness the power of ideas and drive innovation forward.

## ENCOURAGE DIVERGENT THINKING

Encouraging divergent thinking is a powerful way to harness the power of ideas and stimulate creativity. Divergent thinking refers to the ability to generate multiple unique solutions or perspectives to a given problem or question. By embracing divergent thinking, individuals and organizations can unlock new possibilities, promote innovation, and explore alternative approaches.

Foster an atmosphere where individuals feel comfortable expressing their ideas without fear of judgment. Encourage open dialogue, active listening, and respect for different perspectives.

Brainstorming is a classic technique that promotes divergent thinking. Encourage participants to generate as many ideas as possible, focusing on quantity rather than quality during the initial phase. By deferring judgment, participants can freely explore different possibilities.

Actively seek out diverse viewpoints and include individuals from different backgrounds, disciplines, and experiences in idea-generation processes. Diversity of perspectives can lead to fresh insights and novel approaches.

Pose questions that do not have a single correct answer. Open-ended questions stimulate creative thinking by encouraging individuals to explore various possibilities and consider different angles.

Introduce stimuli such as images, articles, or thought-provoking quotes that can inspire new ideas. These stimuli can serve as triggers to prompt unconventional thinking and spur creativity.

Encourage individuals to build upon existing ideas by combining or modifying them. This approach can lead to the generation of novel and innovative concepts.

Foster a culture of curiosity and encourage individuals to explore new territories, experiment, and take risks. Encouraging a growth mindset, where mistakes are viewed as learning opportunities, can help overcome fear of failure and encourage divergent thinking.

Allocate dedicated time for individuals to reflect on ideas, concepts, and problems. This allows for deeper thinking and the development of more creative solutions.

Collaboration can stimulate divergent thinking by leveraging the diverse strengths and perspectives of team members. Encourage collaboration and provide opportunities for individuals to work together and build upon each other's ideas.

Acknowledge and celebrate innovative ideas and creative solutions. Recognition and rewards can motivate individuals to continue thinking divergently and foster a culture that values and supports creative thinking.

By implementing these strategies, individuals and organizations can create an environment that encourages divergent thinking, unlocks the power of ideas, and promotes innovation and creative problem-solving.

## EMBRACE COLLABORATION

Collaboration brings together different perspectives and expertise, leading to the generation of innovative ideas. Encourage teamwork and collaboration across departments, disciplines, and even external partners. Create platforms or spaces where individuals can collaborate, exchange ideas, and build upon each other's contributions.

Ensure that individuals have the necessary resources, tools, and support to transform their ideas into reality. This may include providing access to research materials, funding for prototyping, mentorship, or training programs to enhance skills and knowledge.

Encourage continuous learning and growth within the organization. Promo failures and experimentation, where individuals are encouraged to take risks, learn from failures, and iterate on their ideas. Emphasize the importance of learning from diverse sources, such as industry trends, customer feedback, and external innovations.

Establish mechanisms for gathering feedback on ideas and projects. Encourage constructive criticism and create a safe space for individuals to share their thoughts openly. Feedback helps refine and improve ideas, making them more viable and effective.

Clearly define the goals and priorities for idea generation and implementation. This helps focus efforts and ensures that ideas align with the organization's overall vision and objectives. Provide guidelines and criteria for evaluating ideas to streamline the selection process.

Celebrate and reward individuals or teams that contribute innovative ideas or successfully implement them. Recognition and rewards can range from verbal appreciation, financial incentives, promotions, or opportunities for further development.

Establish formal channels or platforms for idea submission.

This could include suggestion boxes, online forums, or dedicated innovation programs. Encourage regular idea submissions and ensure that they are reviewed and evaluated in a timely manner.

Recognize that the idea generation process is iterative and requires refinement. Continuously assess and improve your idea generation methods based on feedback and outcomes. Learn from both successes and failures to enhance future ideation processes.

Remember, harnessing the power of ideas requires a commitment to nurturing creativity, fostering collaboration, and embracing a culture that values innovation. By following these steps, organizations can unlock the full potential of their ideas and drive meaningful change.

## CULTIVATING AND NURTURING CREATIVE THINKING

Cultivating and nurturing creative thinking is essential for individuals and organizations looking to innovate, solve problems, and stay ahead in today's rapidly changing world.

Encouraging a growth mindset helps individuals believe in their ability to develop and improve their creative thinking skills. This mindset fosters a belief that with effort, practice, and persistence, one can become more creative.

It is crucial to establish an environment where individuals feel safe to express their ideas without fear of judgment or criticism. Encourage open and respectful communication, valuing every individual's contribution. This enables people to take risks and think creatively.

Diversity in terms of backgrounds, experiences, and expertise can significantly enhance creative thinking. Encourage collaboration among people with different skill sets, roles, and viewpoints. This diversity of perspectives can lead to more innovative and varied ideas.

Set aside dedicated time for brainstorming and idea generation. Create opportunities for individuals to step away from their routine tasks and immerse themselves in the creative thinking process. This might include workshops, brainstorming sessions, or designated "thinking time" for individuals to reflect and generate ideas.

Brainstorming is a popular technique for generating ideas. Encourage participants to generate many ideas without judgment or evaluation during the initial phase. Techniques like mind mapping, free writing, or the 6-3-5 method (where six participants generate three ideas each within five minutes) can stimulate creativity and idea flow.

Encourage individuals to ask questions, challenge assumptions, and explore different possibilities. Curiosity is a driving force behind creative thinking. Promote a culture that rewards curiosity and supports experimentation and learning from failures.

Make resources such as books, articles, videos, and online courses on creativity and innovation available to employees. Additionally, expose individuals to diverse sources of inspiration, such as art, nature, or visiting other innovative organizations. Encourage them to attend conferences, workshops, or seminars related to their field.

Once ideas are generated, it is essential to evaluate and refine them. Implement frameworks such as SWOT analysis (strengths, weaknesses, opportunities, threats) or cost-benefit analysis to assess the viability and potential impact of ideas. Encourage constructive feedback and collaboration during this evaluation process.

Allow individuals the autonomy to explore and pursue their ideas. Provide them with the necessary resources, support, and a clear sense of purpose. Autonomy fosters ownership and empowers individuals to bring their creative ideas to life.

Celebrate and recognize individuals who demonstrate creative thinking or produce innovative ideas. This fosters a culture that values and encourages creative contributions, motivating others to think creatively as well.

By implementing these strategies and techniques, and fostering an environment that encourages idea generation, organizations and individuals can enhance their creative thinking capabilities and tap into the vast potential for innovation and problem-solving.

CHAPTER 8

# IDEAS AND PERSONAL GROWTH

I deas and personal growth go hand in hand, as innovative ideas can often spark personal growth and development. There are numerous ways in which ideas can contribute to personal growth.

## STIMULATING CURIOSITY

Stimulating curiosity is an excellent way to foster personal growth. When you're curious about something, it sparks an innate desire to learn, explore, and understand the world around you. This curiosity-driven process opens numerous opportunities for personal development.

Curiosity motivates you to seek answers and learn more about a particular subject. As you delve deeper into a topic that interests you, you acquire knowledge and expand your understanding. This continuous learning enhances your intellectual capabilities and broadens your horizons.

Curiosity encourages you to ask questions and think critically. It enables you to analyze situations, evaluate information, and develop problem-solving skills. Engaging with new ideas and perspectives challenges your existing beliefs, leading to personal growth and development of your cognitive abilities.

Curiosity prompts you to explore different aspects of life, including hobbies, passions, and areas of interest. By exploring new ideas, you gain insights into what truly resonates with you and what aligns with your values. This self-exploration helps you discover your strengths, weaknesses, and personal preferences, ultimately contributing to your personal growth.

Curiosity encourages a growth mindset, which is essential for adaptability and resilience. When you embrace curiosity, you become more open to change, new experiences, and different perspectives. This mindset allows you to adapt to challenges, learn from setbacks, and develop resilience in the face of adversity.

Curiosity is the driving force behind innovation and creativity. When you're curious, you actively seek new ideas, perspectives, and possibilities. This mindset fuels your creativity, enabling you to generate innovative solutions, think outside the box, and find novel approaches to various aspects of life. By nurturing curiosity, you enhance your creative thinking abilities and foster personal growth.

Personal fulfillment and well-being: Engaging with ideas that stimulate curiosity can bring a sense of personal fulfillment and well-being. It adds meaning and purpose to your life, as you pursue your passions and interests. Curiosity encourages a continuous quest for knowledge and personal development, leading to a greater sense of fulfillment and satisfaction.

Stimulating curiosity through engaging with ideas is a powerful catalyst for personal growth. It enhances your knowledge, critical thinking skills, adaptability, resilience, creativity, and overall well-being. Embrace your curiosity, explore new ideas, and let them guide you on a path of self-discovery and continuous growth.

## CHALLENGING EXISTING BELIEFS

Challenging existing beliefs is a fundamental aspect of personal growth, and ideas play a crucial role in facilitating this process.

Ideas introduce us to new concepts, opinions, and perspectives that we may not have encountered before. They provide alternative viewpoints that can challenge our existing beliefs and expand our understanding of the world. By exploring diverse ideas, we gain a broader perspective and become more open-minded.

Engaging with new ideas requires us to critically evaluate our existing beliefs. When we encounter ideas that challenge our current thinking, we are prompted to examine the reasoning behind our beliefs and evaluate their validity. This process fosters critical thinking skills and encourages us to question assumptions.

We all have inherent cognitive biases that shape our perceptions and beliefs. However, exposure to new ideas helps us recognize and overcome these biases. By actively seeking out diverse perspectives and challenging our preconceived notions, we can develop a more objective and nuanced understanding of the world.

Challenging existing beliefs through new ideas can lead to personal development and growth. It encourages self-reflection and introspection, as we evaluate the reasons behind our beliefs and consider alternative possibilities. This process allows us to refine our values, beliefs, and principles, leading to personal growth and a deeper understanding of ourselves.

The ability to adapt and be resilient is essential in a rapidly changing world. By exposing ourselves to new ideas, we become more adaptable and resilient in the face of challenges. Challenging our existing beliefs enables us to embrace change, learn from different perspectives, and adjust our thinking accordingly.

Engaging with new ideas keeps our minds active and intellectually stimulated. It encourages a lifelong learning mindset and a curiosity to explore different subjects. This continuous pursuit of knowledge fosters personal growth by expanding our intellectual capacity and enhancing our overall understanding of the world.

Remember, personal growth is a lifelong journey, and being open to challenging existing beliefs through new ideas is a powerful catalyst for transformation and self-improvement.

## ENCOURAGING CREATIVITY

Ideas play a significant role in personal growth, and they can indeed encourage creativity.

Ideas introduce new concepts and perspectives, challenging our existing beliefs and expanding our worldview. This expansion of knowledge and understanding enables personal growth by broadening our horizons and allowing us to see things from different angles.

Ideas act as catalysts for innovation and creativity. When we encounter new ideas, they spark our imagination and encourage us to think outside the box. This process of exploring alternative possibilities fosters personal growth by fostering problem-solving skills, adaptability, and resourcefulness.

Ideas provide a platform for self-expression. They allow us to articulate our thoughts, feelings, and experiences in unique and imaginative ways. By engaging with different ideas and expressing ourselves creatively, we gain a deeper understanding of our own identity, values, and aspirations, contributing to personal growth and self-discovery.

Ideas serve as a wellspring of knowledge and learning. When we encounter new ideas, we often feel a natural curiosity to explore them further. This pursuit of knowledge leads to continuous learning and personal development. As we engage with diverse ideas, we acquire new skills, expand our intellectual capacity, and enhance our overall personal growth.

Ideas that challenge our comfort zones can be transformative for personal growth. Stepping outside familiar territory and embracing unfamiliar ideas fosters resilience and adaptability. It encourages us to overcome fears, embrace change, and take calculated risks, ultimately leading to personal growth and development.

Engaging with different ideas cultivates open-mindedness and empathy. It helps us appreciate diverse perspectives, challenge biases, and develop a broader understanding of the world. This openness to new ideas nurtures personal growth by fostering tolerance, compassion, and the ability to communicate effectively with others.

Ideas are powerful catalysts for personal growth. By encouraging creativity, expanding perspectives, inspiring innovation, fostering self-expression, encouraging learning, challenging comfort zones, and cultivating open-mindedness, ideas play a vital role in our journey of personal growth and development.

## BUILDING RESILIENCE

Exploring innovative ideas and taking risks can be uncomfortable and even intimidating. However, embracing this discomfort and pushing past your comfort zone can foster resilience. It helps you develop the ability to adapt to change, overcome obstacles, and learn from failures, leading to personal growth and increased confidence. Building resilience is a valuable aspect of personal growth, and ideas can play a significant role in fostering and developing resilience.

Adopting a growth mindset means believing in your ability

to learn and grow through challenges. Embrace the idea that setbacks are opportunities for learning and improvement. Cultivating a growth mindset helps you bounce back from adversity and view obstacles as steppingstones to personal growth.

Take time to reflect on your experiences, both positive and negative. Analyze how you responded to challenges and setbacks and identify areas for improvement. By understanding your emotions, thoughts, and behaviors, you can develop strategies to overcome obstacles and build resilience.

Resilient individuals are adept at finding solutions to problems. Cultivate your problem-solving skills by seeking innovative approaches, considering alternative perspectives, and brainstorming multiple solutions. Embracing the idea that there are multiple paths to success can help you navigate challenging situations more effectively.

Surround yourself with positive, supportive individuals who uplift and encourage you. Share your challenges and seek advice and guidance when needed. Collaborating with others can provide fresh insights and perspectives, and having a support network can help you stay resilient during tough times.

Prioritize self-care as an essential aspect of resilience-building. Take care of your physical, emotional, and mental well-being by practicing healthy habits such as regular exercise, adequate sleep, and balanced nutrition. Engage in activities that bring you joy and relaxation and manage stress effectively through techniques like mindfulness and meditation.

Rather than fearing failure, view it as a chance to learn and grow. Embrace the idea that setbacks are natural and inevitable parts of life. By reframing failure as an opportunity for growth, you can bounce back quicker, adapt to new circumstances, and become more resilient in the face of challenges.

Explore different coping mechanisms that work for you during challenging times. Engage in activities that help you manage stress and regulate your emotions, such as journaling, practicing gratitude, engaging in hobbies, or seeking professional help if needed. The ability to cope effectively with stressors contributes to your overall resilience.

Remember, personal growth and building resilience are ongoing processes. Continuously seek out new ideas, perspectives, and experiences that contribute to your resilience and overall well-being.

## EXPANDING KNOWLEDGE AND SKILLS

Ideas often lead to the acquisition of new knowledge and skills. Engaging with different ideas, whether through reading, conversations, or experiences, broadens your intellectual repertoire. As you learn and acquire new skills, you enhance your personal growth by becoming more knowledgeable and capable.

Ideas challenge our existing beliefs and open new possibilities. By exposing ourselves to different ideas, we expand our understanding of the world and gain fresh perspectives. This broadening of viewpoints helps us grow personally by breaking down preconceived notions and fostering empathy and tolerance.

Ideas introduce us to new concepts, theories, and information. By actively seeking out and engaging with ideas, we continuously learn and acquire knowledge. This process of learning expands our intellectual capacity, enhances our critical thinking skills, and enables us to make more informed decisions in various aspects of life.

Ideas often inspire us to act and develop new skills. Whether it's a new hobby, a professional skill, or a personal interest, ideas push us to learn and grow. By actively pursuing the implementation of ideas, we acquire practical skills, improve our problem-solving abilities, and become more adaptable to change.

Ideas fuel innovation and creativity. When we engage with new ideas, we are prompted to think outside the box, explore novel solutions, and challenge the status quo. This process of innovation fosters personal growth by encouraging us to push boundaries, take calculated risks, and continuously strive for improvement.

Engaging with ideas and expanding our knowledge and skills fosters personal growth by building confidence. As we learn and acquire new information and abilities, we become more self-assured in our capabilities. Confidence allows us to step outside our comfort zones, embrace challenges, and pursue personal and professional growth with determination.

Ideas provide inspiration and motivation for personal development. By exposing ourselves to a variety of ideas, we can identify areas of improvement in our lives and set goals for personal growth. Ideas can offer guidance, strategies, and insights that assist us in becoming the best versions of ourselves.

Ideas are powerful catalysts for personal growth. They expand our knowledge, develop our skills, broaden our perspectives, foster innovation, build confidence, and encourage personal development. Embracing ideas and actively engaging with them can have a transformative effect on our lives and contribute significantly to our overall growth and well-being.

## FOSTERING PERSONAL REFLECTION

Engaging with innovative ideas encourages introspection and self-reflection. By contemplating the implications of

113

different concepts and philosophies, you can gain a deeper understanding of yourself and your values. This self-reflection contributes to personal growth by promoting self-awareness, emotional intelligence, and personal development.

Fostering personal reflection is a powerful way for ideas to contribute to personal growth. When we take the time to reflect on our thoughts, experiences, and beliefs, we create an opportunity for self-awareness, learning, and development. Here's how ideas can contribute to personal growth through fostering personal reflection:

Engaging with new ideas can challenge our existing beliefs and perspectives, prompting us to examine our own thoughts and values. This self-reflection allows us to gain a deeper understanding of ourselves, our motivations, and our biases. By critically evaluating our beliefs considering new ideas, we can expand our self-awareness and identify areas for personal growth.

Exposure to new ideas broadens our horizons and exposes us to different perspectives and experiences. It encourages us to seek out knowledge and explore various subjects. Through personal reflection, we can internalize and integrate these new ideas into our existing knowledge base. This process of continuous learning not only expands our intellectual capacity but also enhances our personal growth and development.

Reflecting on our thoughts and emotions helps us develop emotional intelligence. It allows us to identify and understand our own emotions, as well as the emotions of others. By examining how different ideas or experiences impact our emotional state, we can develop empathy and compassion. This heightened emotional intelligence contributes to personal growth by improving our relationships, decision-making, and overall well-being.

Personal reflection enables us to assess our strengths, weaknesses, and areas of improvement. By evaluating our experiences and progress, we can set meaningful goals and develop strategies to achieve them. Reflecting on our successes and failures helps us learn from past experiences, adjust our approach, and grow as individuals.

Engaging with new ideas and reflecting on them enhances our ability to adapt to change and navigate challenges. By embracing diverse perspectives and exploring alternative solutions, we become more open-minded and flexible in our thinking. Personal reflection allows us to recognize our resilience, learn from setbacks, and cultivate a growth mindset, which is essential for personal growth.

Ideas contribute to personal growth through fostering personal reflection by promoting self-awareness, facilitating learning and knowledge expansion, enhancing emotional intelligence, supporting goal setting and personal development, and fostering resilience and adaptability. By actively engaging with new ideas and reflecting on them, we can unlock our potential for growth and lead more fulfilling lives.

## CONNECTING WITH OTHERS

Engaging in meaningful conversations about ideas can lead to personal growth by broadening your perspective, challenging your assumptions, and deepening your understanding of different viewpoints. Ideas have the power to contribute significantly to personal growth, and one of the most valuable ways they can do so is by connecting individuals with others.

When you encounter new ideas and share them with others, it creates an opportunity to exchange perspectives and broaden your understanding of the world. Engaging in meaningful conversations allows you to gain insights, challenge your own beliefs, and expand your knowledge base.

Ideas can serve as a catalyst for collaboration. By connecting with others who share similar interests or passions, you can form collaborations that lead to mutual growth. Collaborative efforts allow you to pool knowledge, skills, and resources, accelerating personal development and fostering a sense of camaraderie.

Engaging with others who have expertise or experience in areas you aspire to grow can be invaluable. Sharing ideas with mentors or peers who have walked similar paths can provide guidance, encouragement, and support along your personal growth journey. They can offer insights, share strategies, and inspire you to reach new heights.

Sharing ideas can help you build a network of like-minded individuals who share your interests, aspirations, or goals. This network can open doors to new opportunities, whether it's in your personal or professional life. By connecting with others who are passionate about similar ideas, you can find collaborators, mentors, potential employers, or even lifelong friends.

When you share your ideas with others, you invite feedback and constructive criticism. This feedback can help you refine your thoughts, challenge assumptions, and improve your ideas. Engaging in thoughtful discussions and receiving input from others provides a fresh perspective and promotes critical thinking, ultimately contributing to personal growth.

Connecting with others through shared ideas fosters empathy and emotional intelligence. It allows you to understand different viewpoints, appreciate diverse experiences, and develop a more compassionate outlook. These qualities are essential for personal growth, enhancing your ability to navigate relationships, understand yourself, and contribute positively to society.

Ideas play a vital role in personal growth by connecting

individuals with others. Through sharing perspectives, collaborating, seeking support, networking, receiving feedback, and nurturing empathy, ideas create fertile ground for personal development and the expansion of one's horizons.

Overall, ideas serve as catalysts for personal growth by stimulating curiosity, challenging beliefs, encouraging creativity, building resilience, expanding knowledge and skills, fostering reflection, and facilitating social connections. Embracing innovative ideas and being open to intellectual exploration can significantly contribute to your personal growth and development.

Ideas play a crucial role in personal development and self-discovery. They have the power to shape our perspectives, enhance learning, and contribute to the formation of our beliefs, values, and aspirations. By exploring innovative ideas, we expand our understanding of the world and ourselves, opening new possibilities for growth and self-improvement.

Exposure to innovative ideas broadens our perspectives by challenging our existing beliefs and assumptions. When we encounter different viewpoints, cultures, or ways of thinking, we are compelled to reconsider our own perspectives and evaluate them critically. This process allows us to gain a more nuanced understanding of complex issues and encourages empathy and open-mindedness. By embracing diverse ideas, we develop a broader worldview that transcends our limited experiences and fosters a greater appreciation for the richness of human diversity.

Furthermore, exposure to innovative ideas enhances learning by promoting intellectual curiosity and stimulating cognitive development. When we engage with novel concepts, we activate our cognitive processes, such as analysis, synthesis, and evaluation. These mental exercises strengthen our critical thinking skills, problem-solving abilities, and creativity. Learning innovative ideas also fosters a sense of intellectual humility, as it reminds us of the vastness of knowledge and encourages a lifelong pursuit of learning.

Ideas also shape our individual beliefs, values, and aspirations. As we encounter different ideas, we evaluate them considering our existing belief systems, and sometimes, we may find that our beliefs are reinforced or challenged. This process helps us refine and solidify our personal philosophies, leading to a more authentic and coherent sense of self. Ideas can also inspire us to explore new paths, set ambitious goals, and cultivate aspirations aligned with our values and interests.

Moreover, ideas provide us with a framework for understanding the world and our place in it. They offer us a lens through which we interpret and make sense of our experiences. By embracing transformative ideas, we gain insights into societal issues, ethics, and human nature.

This understanding enables us to make informed choices, engage in constructive dialogues, and contribute positively to our communities.

Ideas are catalysts for personal development and self-discovery. They broaden our perspectives, enhance learning, and shape our beliefs, values, and aspirations. Embracing innovative ideas with an open mind allows us to grow intellectually, gain a deeper understanding of the world and ourselves, and lead a more fulfilling and purposeful life.

# CHAPTER 9

# IDEAS AND INNOVATION IN THE DIGITAL AGE

The digital age has revolutionized every aspect of our lives, from communication and entertainment to commerce and healthcare. It has created fertile grounds for ideas and innovation to thrive, offering unprecedented opportunities for individuals and businesses alike.

The internet and advancements in telecommunications have transformed the way we connect and communicate with each other. Social media platforms, messaging apps, and video conferencing tools have bridged the gap between individuals and facilitated the exchange of ideas on a global scale.

The rise of e-commerce has revolutionized the retail industry, enabling businesses to reach customers beyond physical borders. Online marketplaces have opened new avenues for entrepreneurs and small businesses to display and sell their products and services to a vast customer base.

The digital age has witnessed significant advancements in artificial intelligence (AI) and machine learning (ML). These technologies have revolutionized industries such as healthcare, finance, manufacturing, and transportation. They have the potential to automate tasks, enhance decision-making processes, and unlock valuable insights from vast amounts of data.

Streaming platforms, online gaming, and digital content creation have transformed the entertainment industry. The ability to consume and create content anytime, anywhere has empowered individuals and ushered in new opportunities for artists, musicians, filmmakers, and content creators.

The Internet of Things (IoT) refers to the network of interconnected devices that collect and share data. It has opened possibilities for smart homes, wearable devices, industrial automation, and intelligent infrastructure. IoT has the potential to enhance efficiency, improve sustainability, and revolutionize various sectors.

Cloud computing has revolutionized the way businesses store, access, and process data. It provides scalable and flexible infrastructure, reducing the need for extensive on-site hardware and maintenance costs. Cloud computing has paved the way for innovative services such as Software as a Service (SaaS) and Platform as a Service (PaaS).

The digital age has seen a significant transformation in financial services. Fintech startups have introduced innovative solutions for digital payments, peer-to-peer lending, crowdfunding, and cryptocurrency. These advancements have increased financial inclusion and transformed traditional banking processes.

The convergence of healthcare and technology has led to the development of health tech solutions and telemedicine platforms. These in monitoring and improved access to healthcare, allowed remote consultations, facilitated remote patient monitoring, and promoted personalized medicine.

The abundance of data in the digital age has given rise to the field of data analytics. Businesses can leverage data analytics tools to extract valuable insights, make data-driven decisions, and gain a competitive edge. Data-driven innovation has the potential to transform various industries, including marketing, supply chain management, and customer experience.

Digital platforms have enabled collaboration and crowdsourcing of ideas on an unprecedented scale.

Crowdfunding platforms, open-source communities, and collaborative workspaces have brought together diverse talents, facilitating innovation and problem-solving.

These are just a few examples of how ideas and innovation have thrived in the digital age. The rapid pace of technological advancements continues to create new opportunities and challenges, shaping the way we live, work, and interact with the world.

The advent of technology has had a profound impact on idea generation and dissemination, revolutionizing the way information is shared and enabling unprecedented opportunities for innovation. Digital platforms and social media have played a significant role in accelerating the spread of ideas, shaping public opinion, and fostering innovation.

Digital platforms and social media have transformed idea dissemination by providing a global and instantaneous means of communication. Ideas that would have taken days, weeks, or even months to reach a wide audience can now be shared in real-time. This accessibility and speed have democratized the dissemination process, allowing individuals and groups from diverse backgrounds to contribute their ideas and have them reach a potentially large audience.

Moreover, digital platforms and social media have amplified the power of networks and communities, enabling like-minded individuals to connect, collaborate, and exchange ideas. Online communities centered around specific interests or industries have emerged, facilitating knowledge-sharing, brainstorming, and the formation of innovative partnerships. These platforms have also allowed for crowd-based problem-solving, where large groups of people can collectively contribute their expertise to solve complex challenges.

The digital age has presented both challenges and opportunities in fostering innovation. On the one hand, the ease of access to information and the ability to connect with others worldwide has created an environment conducive to idea generation. Innovators can now access a vast pool of knowledge, research, and best practices from across the globe, providing valuable insights that can fuel their creative process.

On the other hand, the sheer volume of information available can be overwhelming and make it difficult to filter out noise from valuable ideas. The speed at which information spreads on digital platforms can also lead to the proliferation of misinformation or the rapid dissemination of unverified ideas. This poses challenges in discerning reliable information and separating innovative ideas from mere hype.

Additionally, the digital age has brought concerns related to privacy, security, and the ethics of data usage. Protecting intellectual property rights and ensuring fair compensation for creators and innovators in the digital realm remains a complex issue. Striking a balance between open collaboration and protecting intellectual property is crucial to foster innovation while incentivizing individuals and organizations to contribute their ideas.

In conclusion, technology, particularly digital platforms, and social media, has significantly influenced the way ideas are generated and disseminated. These platforms have democratized access to information, amplified the power of networks, and facilitated global collaboration. While the digital age presents challenges such as information overload and concerns about privacy and ethics, it also offers immense opportunities for innovation. Balancing the benefits and challenges of the digital age will be essential in creating an environment that fosters and nurtures innovative ideas.

# CHAPTER 10

# IDEAS AND SOCIAL CHANGE

Ideas play a crucial role in driving social change. Throughout history, transformative social movements and shifts in society have often been sparked by innovative ideas that challenge existing norms, promote equality, and advocate for positive change. Here are some ways in which ideas contribute to social change:

New ideas have the power to raise awareness about societal issues and injustices. By highlighting problems and inequalities, they can mobilize individuals and communities to act.

Ideas that challenge prevailing beliefs and ideologies can be catalysts for social change. They encourage critical thinking, questioning the status quo, and promoting alternative perspectives.

Ideas that advocate for the rights and empowerment of marginalized communities can spark social change by giving a voice to those who have been historically oppressed. These ideas can foster solidarity and promote inclusivity.

Ideas centered around equality, justice, and human rights can be transformative in addressing systemic inequalities. They can inspire movements, policies, and practices that strive for a more equitable society.

Innovative ideas can lead to technological advancements, social entrepreneurship, and sustainable solutions that address societal challenges. These ideas can drive economic and social progress while addressing pressing issues such as poverty, climate change, and healthcare.

Ideas that challenge cultural norms and prejudices can reshape societal attitudes and behaviors. They can promote acceptance, tolerance, and understanding across different identities, leading to more inclusive and diverse communities.

Powerful ideas often find their way into policy and legislative changes. Advocacy for innovative ideas can result in the implementation of laws and regulations that promote social justice and protect vulnerable populations.

Ideas that resonate with people's values and aspirations can inspire collective action, including protests, marches, boycotts, and grassroots movements. These actions can bring about social change by putting pressure on institutions and demanding transformative reforms.

It is important to note that ideas alone are not sufficient to bring about social change. Action, organization, and the commitment of individuals and communities are also crucial for turning ideas into tangible outcomes. However, ideas provide the foundation and inspiration for driving social change and creating a more just and inclusive society.

Ideas play a vital role in driving social movements and advocating for change. They have the power to challenge inequality, promote justice, and foster inclusivity. Throughout history, numerous social movements have been sparked by powerful ideas that have ignited passion, mobilized people, and brought about significant transformations in society.

One of the primary ways ideas challenge inequalities is by exposing and critiquing the existing power structures and systems that perpetuate inequity. Ideas can shed light on the structural injustices that marginalize certain groups based on their race, gender, socioeconomic status, or other characteristics. By challenging these systems, ideas can inspire individuals and communities to act, demanding change and equality.

Furthermore, ideas can promote justice by highlighting the injustices faced by marginalized communities and advocating for their rights. Social movements driven by ideas often amplify the voices of those who have been historically silenced or ignored. By articulating their experiences, aspirations, and demands, ideas can drive collective action, mobilizing people to fight for justice and equality.

Inclusivity is another significant aspect influenced by the power of ideas. Ideas that promote inclusivity challenge societal norms and prejudices, fostering a sense of belonging for individuals who have been excluded or discriminated against. These ideas can promote acceptance, tolerance, and understanding across diverse communities, thereby encouraging social cohesion, and creating space for all voices to be heard.

The impact of ideas in driving social change is not limited to their conceptual nature but also extends to their dissemination. Ideas spread through various means such as literature, speeches, media, and now, the internet. The accessibility of information and the ability to engage in discourse have been eased by technological advancements, enabling ideas to reach a wider audience and mobilize more people around a cause.

However, it is important to recognize that the power of ideas alone is not always sufficient to bring about lasting change. Social movements often require strategic planning, organization, and collective action to transform ideas into tangible outcomes. Ideas must be supported by effective advocacy, mobilization efforts, and engagement with policymakers and institutions to translate them into policies, laws, and systemic changes.

Moreover, the impact of ideas can vary depending on the social, cultural, and political context in which they appear. Ideas that challenge inequality, promote justice, and foster inclusivity may face resistance from entrenched interests or ideologies. Overcoming these challenges requires resilience, perseverance, and the ability to adapt strategies to effectively communicate and engage with diverse audiences.

In conclusion, the power of ideas to drive social movements and advocate for change is undeniable. Ideas challenge inequality by exposing systemic injustices, promote justice by amplifying marginalized voices, and foster inclusivity by challenging societal norms. However, for ideas to translate into transformative action, they must be supported by strategic planning, collective action, and engagement with institutions. The role of ideas in shaping society and advancing social progress should be acknowledged and harnessed to create a more just and inclusive world.

# CHAPTER 11

# IDEAS AND GLOBAL COLLABORATION

I deas and global collaboration can be incredibly powerful forces for positive change in the world. When people from diverse backgrounds, cultures, and perspectives come together to share ideas and work towards a common goal, amazing things can happen.

Global collaboration brings together individuals with diverse backgrounds, experiences, and knowledge. This diversity of perspectives can lead to innovative ideas and solutions that may not have been possible within a single cultural or geographical context. Different viewpoints can challenge assumptions, spark creativity, and foster unique approaches to problem-solving.

Collaboration across borders eases the sharing of knowledge and expertise. People can learn from each other's experiences, best practices, and unique insights. This exchange of knowledge can lead to accelerated learning, improved decision-making, and the development of modern technologies or methodologies.

Many of the world's most pressing challenges, such as climate change, poverty, healthcare disparities, and education gaps, require collaborative efforts. By working together on a global scale, individuals and organizations can pool resources, share research findings, and implement coordinated strategies to address these complex problems effectively.

Global collaboration often sparks innovation and fosters creativity. When individuals from diverse cultures and backgrounds come together, they bring their unique perspectives and approaches to the table. This blending of ideas can lead to breakthrough innovations, novel solutions, and transformative changes in various fields, including science, technology, arts, and social initiatives.

Global collaboration supplies a platform for individuals and groups who may have been historically marginalized or underrepresented to have their voices heard. It promotes inclusivity, equality, and diversity, ensuring that a wide range of perspectives and ideas are considered and valued.

Collaborating on a global scale allows individuals and organizations to build strong networks and establish connections across borders. These connections foster ongoing relationships, partnerships, and collaborations, which can lead to long-term positive impact and the exchange of ideas beyond a single project or initiative.

Global collaboration allows for the pooling of resources, both financial and intellectual. By combining expertise, funding, and infrastructure, collaborators can amplify their impact and achieve outcomes that may not have been possible individually. This collective approach enables projects to scale up, reach broader audiences, and create more sustainable solutions.

To foster ideas and global collaboration effectively, it is crucial to establish platforms, networks, and initiatives that facilitate communication, knowledge sharing, and cooperation. This can include international conferences, research partnerships, cross-cultural exchange programs, virtual collaboration platforms, and funding mechanisms that support global initiatives. It is also important to promote diversity, inclusivity, and equitable participation to ensure that all voices are heard and valued.

By embracing ideas and global collaboration, we can tap

into the collective wisdom of humanity and work together to address the world's challenges, create positive change, and build a more inclusive and sustainable future.

The role of ideas in fostering collaboration across borders and cultures is paramount. Ideas serve as the building blocks for innovation, understanding, and problem-solving. When shared and exchanged between individuals from diverse backgrounds and cultures, ideas can transcend boundaries and facilitate collaboration on a global scale.

Firstly, ideas play a crucial role in breaking down barriers and fostering mutual understanding. When people from diverse cultures and countries come together to share their ideas, they bring diverse perspectives, experiences, and knowledge. This exchange of ideas helps to bridge cultural gaps, challenge preconceived notions, and promote empathy and openness. By engaging in open and respectful dialogue, individuals can learn from one another, appreciate different viewpoints, and develop a deeper understanding of the issues at hand.

Secondly, shared ideas are instrumental in addressing global challenges. Many of the complex problems we face today, such as climate change, poverty, and healthcare, require collaborative efforts across borders. By exchanging ideas and best practices, countries and cultures can pool their collective knowledge and resources to find innovative and effective solutions. Through collaboration, ideas can be refined, expanded upon, and tailored to suit different contexts, leading to more comprehensive and sustainable approaches to global challenges.

Furthermore, shared ideas have the power to inspire and motivate individuals and communities. When people witness the impact and success of ideas implemented in various parts of the world, it creates a ripple effect of innovation and collaboration. Ideas can transcend geographical boundaries and cultural differences, sparking enthusiasm and collective action towards common goals. This shared sense of purpose and inspiration can fuel collaborative efforts and enable individuals from diverse backgrounds to work together towards a common vision.

It is worth noting that the effective exchange and implementation of ideas across borders and cultures require certain conditions. Open communication channels, inclusive platforms, and a willingness to embrace diversity are essential. Additionally, efforts should be made to ensure equal participation and representation from all stakeholders involved. By fostering an environment that values and encourages the sharing of ideas, collaboration can flourish and contribute to meaningful global progress.

The role of ideas in fostering collaboration across borders and cultures cannot be overstated. Shared ideas promote understanding, break down barriers, and provide the foundation for addressing global challenges. By engaging in dialogue, exchanging knowledge, and drawing on diverse perspectives, individuals and communities can collaborate effectively and contribute to a more interconnected and harmonious world.

# CHAPTER 12

# THE FUTURE OF IDEAS

The future of ideas is a broad and complex topic, as it encompasses the evolution of human creativity, innovation, and intellectual property in a rapidly changing world. While I cannot predict the specifics of the future, I can provide insights and potential trends based on the current trajectory of ideas and knowledge.

**Collaboration and Open Innovation:** The future is likely to see increased collaboration and open innovation. As communication and connectivity technologies continue to advance, people from diverse backgrounds and locations can come together to share ideas and work on projects collectively. Open-source software, crowdsourcing platforms, and collaborative platforms have already demonstrated the power of collective intelligence, and this trend is expected to grow.

**Digital Transformation:** The ongoing digital revolution will continue to shape the future of ideas. With the increasing integration of technology into our daily lives, ideas will be generated, shared, and consumed in digital formats. The internet, social media, and online platforms provide unprecedented opportunities for individuals to express their creativity and share their ideas with a global audience.

**Artificial Intelligence (AI) and Automation:** AI technologies are poised to play a significant role in the future of ideas. AI can assist in generating ideas, analyzing large datasets, and making connections across various fields. Automated systems can aid in idea generation and provide valuable insights to creators. However, there are also concerns about AI's impact on creativity and originality, as it raises questions about the authenticity and uniqueness of ideas generated by machines.

**Intellectual Property and Legal Frameworks:** As innovative ideas emerge; intellectual property laws and frameworks will need to adapt. Issues surrounding copyright, patents, and ownership will become more complex in a digital and globally interconnected world.

Striking a balance between protecting the rights of creators and fostering innovation and creativity will be an ongoing challenge.

**Ethical and Social Considerations:** The future of ideas will undoubtedly involve ethical and social considerations. As innovative technologies and ideas emerge, ethical dilemmas may arise concerning their impact on society, privacy, and human values. Discussions around AI ethics, data privacy, and the responsible use of emerging technologies will be crucial in shaping the future of ideas.

**Interdisciplinary Approaches:** The boundaries between different fields of knowledge are becoming increasingly blurred. Interdisciplinary approaches and collaborations between diverse disciplines are likely to result in novel and innovative ideas. Fields such as biotechnology, nanotechnology, artificial intelligence, and renewable energy will intersect, leading to new discoveries and transformative ideas.

Ultimately, the future of ideas will depend on the collective actions and choices made by individuals, communities, and societies. As technology continues to advance and our understanding of the world deepens, it is essential to foster an environment that encourages creativity, collaboration, and the responsible exploration of ideas.

Emerging fields of research often bring forth powerful ideas that have the potential to shape the future in profound ways. These ideas can revolutionize various aspects of our lives, ranging from technology and medicine to social sciences and environmental sustainability. However, along with their transformative potential, these ideas also raise important ethical implications and responsibilities that must be carefully considered.

One emerging field with significant potential is artificial intelligence (AI) and machine learning. As AI becomes increasingly sophisticated, it opens new possibilities for automation, data analysis, and decision-making. While this offers numerous benefits, such as improved efficiency and productivity, it also raises ethical concerns. For instance, there are concerns about the impact of AI on job displacement, privacy and data security, algorithmic bias, and the potential for AI systems to make decisions that may have harmful consequences.

Another promising area is genetic engineering and gene editing technologies, such as CRISPR-Cas9. These technologies hold tremendous potential for treating genetic diseases, enhancing food production, and even modifying human traits. However, they also raise ethical questions about the boundaries of manipulating nature and human life. Issues like genetic discrimination, unintended consequences, and the equitable distribution of benefits and risks need to be carefully addressed.

The field of neuroethics, which explores the ethical implications of advancements in neuroscience, is also gaining attention. As our understanding of the brain improves, it raises questions about the privacy of thoughts, the potential for mind control, cognitive enhancement, and the nature of personal identity. Researchers and policymakers need to ensure that neuroscientific advancements are guided by ethical principles, protecting individual autonomy, and avoiding undue influence or manipulation.

Climate change and sustainable development represent another crucial area of research. As the world grapples with the environmental crisis, innovative ideas and technologies are needed to mitigate the impacts and transition to a sustainable future. However, the responsible development and deployment of these ideas is paramount. This involves considering the social and economic implications of environmental policies, ensuring equitable access to resources and technologies, and respecting the rights and knowledge of Indigenous communities.

Emerging fields of research also raise broader societal and philosophical questions. For instance, developments in the field of consciousness studies challenge our understanding of the mind and the nature of subjective experience. As we explore the frontiers of physics and cosmology, concepts like the multiverse and the nature of time challenge our fundamental conceptions of reality.

Considering these powerful ideas, it is essential for researchers, policymakers, and society to embrace their ethical responsibilities. Open and inclusive discussions, involving interdisciplinary perspectives and public engagement, can help navigate the ethical implications of emerging fields. Ethical guidelines and regulations should be developed to ensure responsible research practices, transparency, and accountability. Additionally, there should be ongoing evaluation and assessment of the societal impact of these powerful ideas, allowing for adaptive governance and responsible innovation.

In conclusion, emerging fields of research bring forth powerful ideas that have the potential to shape the future in profound ways. While these ideas hold tremendous promise, it is vital to acknowledge and address the ethical implications and responsibilities associated with them. By doing so, we can ensure that the transformative power of these ideas is harnessed for the greater benefit of humanity while mitigating potential risks and negative consequences.

# CONCLUSION

In the vast tapestry of human history, there is a force that has shaped civilizations, toppled empires, and transformed the world as we know it. It is a force that knows no bounds, transcending time, and space to ignite the flames of progress and ignite the embers of revolution. It is the power of ideas.

Throughout this journey, we have explored the profound impact that ideas have had on our lives. From the ancient philosophers who dared to question the nature of reality to the modern innovators who push the boundaries of what is possible, the power of ideas has been a driving force behind human advancement.

Ideas possess an incredible ability to inspire, motivate, and mobilize. They have the power to unite disparate minds under a common cause and fuel the flames of change. Whether it is the idea of freedom that ignited revolutions or the idea of equality that shattered barriers, it is through the power of ideas that we have witnessed the greatest shifts in human history.

Yet, ideas are not without their challenges. They can be met with resistance, rejection, and skepticism. They can be seen as dangerous, disruptive, and destabilizing. However, it is precisely in the face of adversity that ideas find their true strength. They persist, they evolve, and they adapt. They have the power to overcome even the most formidable obstacles, paving the way for a better future.

The power of ideas extends beyond the realm of academia and intellectual discourse. It infiltrates every aspect of our lives, from science and technology to art and culture, from politics and governance to personal beliefs and values. It is the catalyst for innovation, progress, and human flourishing.

But with great power comes great responsibility. As custodians of ideas, we must wield this power with care and integrity. We must nurture a culture that encourages the free exchange of ideas, embracing diversity and inclusivity. We must challenge our own biases and preconceptions, opening ourselves to new perspectives and possibilities. And we must recognize the potential consequences of our ideas and strive for ethical, sustainable, and equitable outcomes.

The power of ideas is not limited to a select few; it resides within each one of us. We are all capable of generating ideas that can transform our lives and the lives of others. By embracing our creativity, curiosity, and imagination, we tap into this limitless reservoir of potential.

As we conclude this exploration into the power of ideas, let us remember that ideas have the power to shape the world. They can create, they can disrupt, and they can inspire. The true measure of their power lies in how we choose to use them. So, let us dare to dream, to question, and to imagine a better world. Let us harness the power of ideas to forge a future that is just, compassionate, and filled with boundless possibilities.

# ABOUT THE AUTHOR

Robert Osobase has a Bachelor of Philosophy, Master of Social Work, and Doctoral degree in Healthcare Administration. He has worked in the healthcare industry since arriving the United States in 2007. The knowledge of the field of Philosophy and studying the bible has provided him with the foundation to understand the values and principles that underpin strategies for overcoming the devices of the enemy. Robert currently resides in Arlington, Texas.